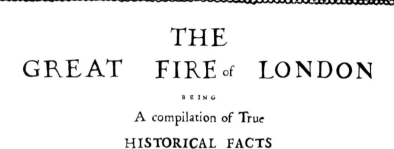

THE
GREAT FIRE of LONDON

BEING

A compilation of True

HISTORICAL FACTS

AND

Archaeological Evidence newley difcovered

OF THE

LATE DREADFUL CONFLAGRATION

WHICH

CONSUMED our CAPITAL CITY

In 1666

Touching alfo upon the magnificence of the Rebuilding thereafter

The
GREAT FIRE
of LONDON

Gustav Milne

HISTORICAL PUBLICATIONS LTD

ISBN 0 9503656 9 6

Typeset by Phoenix Photosetting, Chatham
Printed in Hong Kong by
The South China Printing Company

Published by
Historical Publications Ltd
54 Station Road
New Barnet, Herts
(01–607 1628)

ILLUSTRATIONS

Permission to reproduce the following illustrations was kindly given by the Museum
of London: 6, 9, 13, 17, 21, 23, 24, 27, 32, 35, 36, 45, 50, 51, 56, 61, 62, 64, 65, 67, 68 and
the cover.

Permission to reproduce the following illustrations was kindly given by the Guildhall
Library: 7, 10, 29.

All other illustrations are from the collection of Historical Publications Ltd.

The cover illustration is from a painting owned by the Museum of London, by an
unknown Dutch artist.

CONTENTS

ABOUT THE AUTHOR

Gustav Milne has worked for the Museum of London's Archaeological Department since its inception in 1973, and has excavated on many sites in the City of London including Trig Lane, Pudding Lane, Billingsgate and the Roman Basilica site at Leadenhall Court. He has published reports in many local and national journals and has lectured widely in this country and abroad. He obtained a degree of Master of Philosophy from the University of London in 1985 for a thesis on medieval waterfront installations in the City. His publications include:

D. Andrews and Gustav Milne, *Wherram: A Study of Settlement on the Yorkshire Wolds*, Volume 1: *Domestic Settlement*. Society of Medieval Archaeology Monograph No 8 (1979).
Gustav Milne and Brian Hobley, *Waterfront Archaeology in Britain and Northern Europe*. Council for British Archaeology Research Report No 41 (1981).
Gustav Milne and Christine Milne, *Medieval Waterfront Development at Trig Lane, London*. London and Middlesex Archaeological Society Special Paper No 5 (1982).
Gustav Milne, *The Port of Roman London* (Batsford 1985).

ACKNOWLEDGEMENTS

This book has benefited from the work of many people, as the references in the footnotes show, and from the discussions and advice of several friends and colleagues, in particular John Richardson of Historical Publications, Alison Blake and Christine Milne, who also drew the maps and diagrams for this publication. Many illustrations are reproduced by kind permission of the Museum of London, and include several supplied by the Department of Urban Archaeology's photographic unit.

In this book, the spelling and place-names adopted in the transcripts of the 17th-century documents have been modernised for the sake of clarity. Any mistakes or misinterpretations in these sections or elsewhere in the text remain the author's responsibility.

1. Part of London, as it appeared during the dreadful fire of 1666.

This book is dedicated to Alan, Alexis, Ben, Debbie, Michelle, Owen, Peta, Reuben and Sharon.

Introduction

'The most destructive fire England has ever seen' . . . was how one eye-witness described the conflagration that raged in London from the 2nd to the 6th of September, 1666. It had a devastating effect on the old medieval City and its 17th century citizens and still continues to exercise a powerful hold on the imagination. There have been more horrific fires in our own century, but, in terms of damage to the City itself, not even the Blitz in the 1940s caused as much destruction. The mystical date of 1666 and the infamous address of the King's Bakehouse in Pudding Lane remain universal synonyms for the event which is still known as THE Great Fire of London.

Naturally, this important event and its aftermath has attracted the attention of distinguished historians, notably W. G. Bell, who published his '*Great Fire of London*' in 1920 and T. F. Reddaway, whose '*Rebuilding of London after the Great Fire*' appeared, rather ironically, in 1940. What is perhaps surprising is that no major studies have appeared subsequently. The aim of this book is to provide a modern review of historical and archaeological evidence in an accessible form to complement their detailed work.

In Part One, London is seen on the eve of the Fire, recovering from the effects of Civil War and the Plague which decimated its population in 1665. Part Two is a collection of eye-witness accounts of the Fire, arranged so as to form a Chronicle of the Fire itself. The writers include not only the famous diarists Samuel Pepys and John Evelyn, but also two protestant preachers Edward Waterhouse and Thomas Vincent, whose descriptions of the Fire are also published here in detail. Of all these, the account by Thomas Vincent is the most graphic but, surprisingly, is the least well-known. In addition, extracts from contemporary letters, such as those written by Wind. Sandys who was with the Duke of York (later James II) at the time of the Fire, from the Parliamentary Inquiry into the causes of the Fire, Public Records Office, and from the *London Gazette* published on 8th September 1666 are also utilised. The narrative thus produced makes compelling reading, for the differing styles and viewpoints provide an alarmingly vivid picture of the Fire's progress. The text is illustrated by contemporary prints and pictures, and also with a series of photographs of the fire-damaged buildings themselves. This evocative photographic record of an event which took place two centuries

1666

1939-45

0   1km

before the advent of photography is result of recent archaeological work by the Museum of London.

After the Great Fire came the Great Rebuilding, and this is summarised in Part Three, while Part Four presents a review of archaeological evidence of the disaster. For example, in the cold winter of 1979/80 the Museum of London excavated several trenches on a site in Pudding Lane. Here, in the shadow of the Monument, substantial remains of a fire-blackened building were discovered and recorded. The graphic glimpse back in time to September 1666 which this provided was the initial inspiration for this book. A less welcome stimulus was the outbreak of a major fire in the house where the illustrator of this book lived. The lower storeys of the building were engulfed in flames and choking smoke within minutes of this fire starting, and she and the cat only escaped by climbing out onto the roof, just like the baker's family had to do in Pudding Lane 320 years earlier. Luckily the modern fire was quickly brought under control by the Fire Brigade, and even the artwork was saved. However, the courage and efficiency of such professional fire fighters were sorely lacking in 1666.

2. How great was the Great Fire of 1666? These plans of the City of London compare areas of devastation (shown shaded] caused by the Great Fire (top) with damage inflicted on the area within the ancient City walls during the Blitz in 1939–45. (C. Milne)

In sum, this book brings together for the first time both the basic historical and archaeological evidence of that sad event and its aftermath. In so doing, it became clear that some aspects of the folk-lore of the Fire required re-examination and reassessment. For example, it is widely believed that Pepys's diary provides the best account of the disaster; that Charles II played a central, heroic role in saving London; and also that the rebuilding after the Fire was a wasted opportunity, since Wren's plan for the City was not adopted.

The first point is most easily assessed by comparing all the accounts published in Part Two. Considered on its own, Pepys's description gives a very narrow view of the Fire, and its true value is only appreciated when balanced by the comments of the other eye-witnesses.

Of greater importance is the role played by Charles II, eulogised by many writers from Dryden to Bell, and enshrined in the allegorical panels on the base of the Monument itself. However, his actions during the whole episode seem to have been motivated primarily by a desire to prevent civil unrest and potential revolution after the Fire, ie, saving his own crown rather than the saving of the City for its own sake. One of the most telling documents on this score is the letter written on the Tuesday from Lord Arlington on behalf of the King and council, to Sir Thomas Clifford. In it, Clifford is asked to persuade the Duke of Albemarle to return from fighting the Dutch. The popular Duke was the man who offered Charles II the crown in 1660 at the Restoration. Such was the gravity of the crisis in 1666 that it was suggested the Duke 'will have it in his own hands to give the King his kingdoms a second time'. Charles, realising that the Great Fire could rekindle the Great Rebellion, took every precaution to maintain law and order in the aftermath of the disaster. In any case, it was in his best long-term interests that the City rose promptly, peacefully and prosperously from the ashes of September 1666. If London, the largest town in the land, was allowed to go to the wall, then the Stuarts would surely follow.

The third point is dealt with in Part Three, in which it is argued that the City which was elegantly planned and speedily rebuilt after the Fire was a masterly example of town-planning in the most adverse of circumstances.

The story of the Great Fire is tragic, and continues to capture the imagination. But the Monument, still standing sentinel on Fish Street Hill (the road to Old London Bridge) does not so much commemorate that disaster as London's miraculous recovery. The greater the tragedy, the greater our admiration should be for those who rose above it: by the last decade of the 17th century, London ultimately triumphed over the Great Fire of London.

3. John Evelyn (1620–1706). His Diary contains one of the eye-witness accounts of the Great Fire.

Opposite:
4. Samuel Pepys (1633–1703). Pepys was actually living in the City when the Fire broke out in September 1666. Like the majority of the inhabitants, he chose to pack his valuables and flee rather than fight the Fire.

John Evelyn Esq.ʳ

Samuel Pepys Esq. Secretary to the Admiralty.

Painted by Sir Godfrey Kneller

Your faithful and obed. Ser.

Derby House 27. April 1690.

His Autograph from an original Letter
in the possession of John Thane.

PART ONE

A CONGESTION OF MIS-SHAPEN HOUSES:
London before the Fire

Population and Plague

On Saturday 1st September 1666, the eve of the Great Fire, unsuspecting London lay cramped and crowded within its medieval walls with open fields to the north and east, the wide Thames flowing to the south, and a rich suburb expanding westwards towards Whitehall and Westminster.[1] The City itself 'with its 109 churches rising amidst the timber-framed houses and innumerable gables, the steel-grey fortress of the Tower at the watergate and palaces beyond, was a delight to the eye', in the words of the distinguished historian Walter Bell. However, those who had to live there were also well aware of its shortcomings, for it was as famous 'for its dirt, overcrowding, squalor and general unwholesomeness'.[2] The Plague thrived in such conditions, killing over 25,000 Londoners in both 1603 and 1625, and 10,000 in 1636.[3] London's population was therefore subject to considerable fluctuations throughout the period before the Fire, and recent research suggests that it was substantially larger in 1300 (before the Black Death) than it was in 1500.[4] Subsequently the City and its suburbs expanded to house a population of 120,000 in 1550, 200,000 by 1600 and 375,000 by 1650.[5]

But in an address to parliament in 1661, John Evelyn had declared:

that this glorious and ancient City . . . should wrap her stately head in clouds of smoke and sulphur, so full of stink and darkness, I deplore with just indignation. That the buildings should be composed of such a congestion of mis-shapen and extravagant houses, that the streets should be so narrow and incommodious in the very centre . . ., that there should be so ill and uneasy a form of paving underfoot, so troublesome and malicious a disposure of the spouts and gutters overhead, are particulars worthy of reproof.[6]

Four years later, 70,000 citizens of this insanitary City had died wretchedly after the last visitation of the Plague.

Politics, Puritans and Papists

People of John Evelyn's generation (he was born in 1620) would also have witnessed great political and religious upheaval during their lifetime. The troubled 17th century saw the Midlands Revolt in 1607, the Western Rising in 1628–30 and the Civil War in the 1640s. After 1642 London played a central

7. Hogenburg's map of London 1572. *The map shows the Elizabethan city enclosed by its walls, its suburbs spreading out over the surrounding fields. The Fire of 1666 destroyed many of the buildings shown here.*

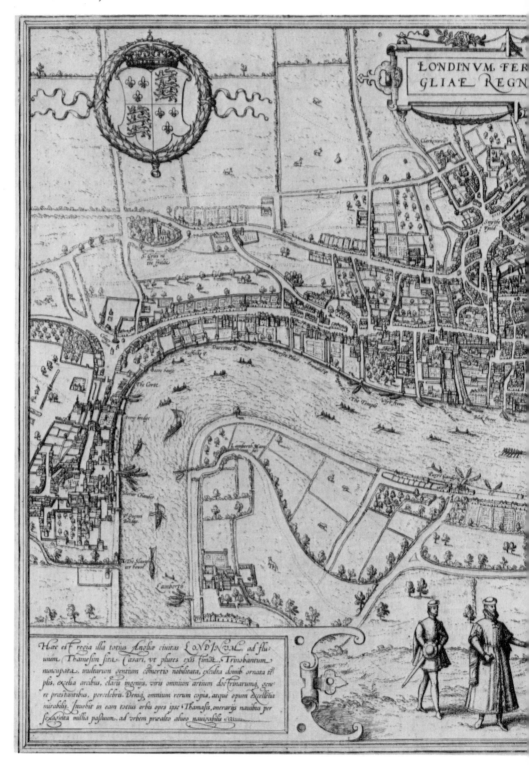

8. Charles II
(1630–1685)

role for the Parliamentary forces against the King, when power in the City
was seized by their supporters.[7] With London on their side, they held a major
port and the wealthiest town in the land. At the close of the Civil War, London
was on the winning side, a fact which did not endear its citizens to the later
Stuart Kings. Charles I was executed as a traitor in Whitehall in 1649, after
which the Commonwealth was established in 1653.

Although the monarchy was restored in 1660 in the person of Charles II,
discontent resurfaced with such events as Venner's Rising in 1661 and the
Derwentdale Plot in 1663. Meanwhile, in the Channel and overseas, there
were wars against the Dutch, the French, the Spanish and the Irish. Indeed, at
the time of the Fire, the English fleet was actively engaged in chasing and
fighting the Dutch, following the burning of 160 enemy ships during the
successful attack on the islands of Vlie and Schelling on 8th August 1666.

As for Charles II, his position on the eve of the Fire was by no means secure.
His insecurity was well-founded, for just three months after the Fire for
example, there was a rising in Scotland which was brutally put down by the
army, leaving 500 dead on the Pentland Hills. His successor the, catholic
James II, would be confronted with Monmouth's Rebellion in 1685, and
would be deposed in the Glorious Revolution led by the protestant William of

Orange in 1688. It was therefore the spectre of extensive civil unrest following the Fire, rather than the disaster itself, which motivated most of Charles' actions in September, 1666. He was well aware that large demonstrations and riots were commonplace in 17th century London, a town which Samuel Rolle described as 'the great bulwark and fortress of protestant interest',[8] and which therefore distrusted kings with catholic sympathies.

Many of these turbulent themes are met with in the Fire Chronicle in Part 2 and the Diary of Redevelopment in Part 3, compilations of contemporary accounts in which the widely diverging politics, social class and religious fervour of the 17th century writers is eloquently apparent. In their reports, the friction between classes, between 'puritans' and 'papists', between Londoners and foreigners burns as fiercely as the fire itself.

City Life
By contrast, the buildings and streets which formed the fabric of the City itself had seen little major change in that half century before the Fire. In fact John Evelyn's parents, and even his grandparents, would have recognised much of London had they been able to return to it in the mid-17th century. It was in most essentials the town described by John Stow in his famous survey

9. A congestion of mis-shapen houses. The streets and narrower lanes of London on the eve of the Fire were lined with timber-framed buildings packed closely together, as this model of a street off Cheapside shows

19

published in 1603.[9] City life was still organised and administered by parish, ward and gild. London's medieval skyline was dominated by 109 churches, representing the subdivision of the City into smaller, more intimate parish communities, almost like villages within the town. For administrative purposes, the town was also divided into twenty-six wards, which elected aldermen who, with the Lord Mayor, governed London. Their presence was symbolised by the magnificent Guildhall, which stood in the north-west part of the town.

The commercial life of London was in the hands of the many companies whose splendid halls were such a noteworthy feature of the City. There were some 100 gilds in London, and they exercised considerable control over all aspects of trading and manufacturing in the capital. Among the most important of these restrictions was their insistence upon a seven-year apprenticeship before granting the freedom to ply a particular trade in the London area.

As a direct result of such restrictions, new businesses often set up in the areas outside the walls, where the long arm of the gilds could not always reach them. These suburbs were developing at a dramatic rate in the mid-17th century. London's rising population was due almost entirely to a vast influx of migrants from the poorer rural areas of England, rather than from a rising birth rate. By the early 17th century the northern and eastern suburbs were growing the fastest, and were occupied mainly by artisans and small industries. The western suburb began to develop at speed in the mid-17th century, providing services and luxury items for the capital.[10] The trades and crafts practised in the suburbs differed from those in the City only in that there was a much larger concentration of merchants and professions within the ancient walls.

In the City itself, surrounding the medieval churches, company halls and other public buildings, were streets, lanes and alleys crowded with tall, timber-framed buildings. M. J. Power's detailed study of the hearth tax returns for 1660–6 (a tax on buildings assessed on the number of fireplaces each had) has thrown interesting light on the topography of the pre-Fire town. Four kinds of public way are distinguished in the returns, streets, lanes, yards and alleys. A 'street' was a major thoroughfare, possibly paved, flanked by large houses (from five to nine hearths) often occupied by victuallers, dealers or the professional classes. A 'lane' was narrower, with smaller houses (four to five hearths) occupied by metal and wood craftsmen. A 'yard' or court was an enclosed space entered by a turning off a street or lane, flanked by slightly smaller buildings (four hearths), and, like the even smaller buildings off an 'alley' (only three to four hearths), were usually occupied by builders, carriers, or textile and leather craftsmen.[11]

Further work on documentary sources, in this case for a group of properties near Cheapside, provides more details of life in pre-Fire London, and may well be typical of the general pattern. Dr Keene has shown that, in the early 17th century, rich and poor lived virtually side by side in the City, but the wealthiest inhabitants occupied secluded spacious sites set back from the street frontage. The houses of artisans and shopkeepers opened directly onto the road, but had little space for a garden or yard behind. The poorest inhabitants lived in single rooms, usually in an upper storey. A typical London house of this period would have a cellar; a ground floor containing a shop, workshop or store; a second storey with the dining rooms and kitchens; the sleeping accommodation on the floor above with a garret over that.[12]

Fighting Fires

Fires breaking out in such a densely occupied town were not uncommon; as long ago as the late 12th century, William Fitzstephen had complained that the only inconveniences of London were the immoderate drinking of the foolish and the frequency of fires. In 1632, a considerable area around the northern end of Old London Bridge was burnt down, but any lessons learned from that experience were not recalled thirty-four years later. The danger was appreciated, but all warnings went unheeded. In 1661 John Evelyn drew Parliament's attention to the risk run by the City and even the King wrote to the Lord Mayor of London in 1664 to recommend the more diligent execution of recent building legislation 'to preserve that great and prosperous City from Fire'.[13]

The standard method of dealing with such problems remained the same: there were no fire brigades organised by civic authorities nor even by insurance companies as was to be the case in the 18th century. Such matters were considered to be local concerns, and were thus the responsibility of the community at street, parish or ward level. A compilation of parish officers, duties, published after the Great Fire, but describing traditional arrangements for coping with such emergencies simply states that '. . . on the breaking out of a fire, all constables and beadles shall repair to the place with their staves and assist in putting out the flame, and causing people to work . . .'.[14] To this end, leather buckets, ladders, axes, ropes and the large iron fire-hooks used to drag timber-framed buildings to the ground were supposedly kept in every

10. Few fire-fighting devices existed in the 17th century. The water-squirt, shown in this illustration, was ineffective in large fires.

City church and at some of the Livery Company halls. Hoses were unknown, although there are in the Museum of London collection some late 17th century primitive metal squirts which contained less than a gallon of water. The 'water-engines' mentioned in the contemporary accounts of the Great Fire would have been more useful: these were large movable water tanks, often with a pump attachment.

Traditional fire-fighting practices included the pulling down of buildings in the path of the flames to provide a fire-break which could contain the blaze. However, since compensation was payable to the owner of the property thus demolished, such descisions could not be made lightly or quickly. Indeed in September 1666, the Londoners, inability to clear adequate fire-breaks at the start of the conflagration had disastrous consequences. In the 17th century, the fastest way to dismantle a timber-framed building was to explode a charge of gunpowder just sufficient to dislodge the superstructure from its foundations, causing the framework to collapse. The timbers could then be hauled off the site away from the flames. Although this method should have been known to the authorities in London (the sailors certainly knew of it), it does not seem to have been used until the third day of the Fire: London paid dearly for this delay. This then, was the level of technology and organisation which Londoners had to draw on to fight the Fire.

Prophets of Doom

London ultimately rose above adversity, above a disaster which could have been prevented as certainly as, in a superstitious age, it had been predicted. A selection of these remarkable prophecies[15] is presented below together with the dates when they were originally published as a fitting preface to the Fire Chronicle itself.

1641:   A ship come sailing up the Thames to London- and the master of the ship shall weep, and the mariners shall aske him why he weepeth, being that he hath made so good a voyage, and he shall say 'Ah, what a goodly City this was, none in the world comparable to it; and now there is scarcely left any house that can let us have a drink for our money'
Mother Shipton's Prophecies

1658:   London, go on still in thy presumptuous wickedness! Put the evil day far from thee, and repent not! Do so London. But if fire make not ashes of the City, and thy bones also, conclude me a liar for ever. Oh, London! London! Sinful as Sodom and Gomorrah! The decree is gone out, Repent, or burn, as Sodom, as Gomorrah!
Walter Gostelo: *The Coming of God in Mercy, in Vengeance, beginning with Fire, to convert or consume all this so sinful City London*

1659:   A consuming fire shall be kindled in the bowels of the earth . . . Yea, a great effusion of blood, fire and smoke shall increase up in the dark habitations of cruelty, howling and great wailing shall be on every hand in all her streets.
Daniel Baker: *Certaine Warning for a Naked Heart*

1660: And as for the City, herself and her suburbs and all that belonging to her, a fire was kindled therein . . . and there was none could quench it . . . and it consumed all the lofty things therein, and the fire searched out all hidden places and burned most of her state to be very miserable, and very few were those who were left in her . . . And the fire continued for, though all the lofty part was brought down, yet there was much old stuff and parts of broken down desolate walls which the fire continued burning against. And the vision thereof remained in me as a thing that was showed me of the Lord.

Humphrey Smith: *Vision which he saw concerning London*

In April 1666, a papist plot to burn the City was foiled and the plotters captured and hanged. The date they had set for their attack was, remarkably, Monday 3rd September, since it was claimed that the stars predicted a major disaster on that day. The stars are also mentioned in a report by Daniel Defoe, published in 1722. In his account of the events of 1665 and 1666, he claims that '. . . a blazing star or comet appeared for several months before the Plague, as there did the year after another, a little before the Fire. I saw both these stars and I must confess had so much of the common notion of such things in my head that I was apart to look upon them as the forerunners and warnings of God's judgement, especially when, after the Plague had followed the first [comet] I yet saw another of the like kind, I could not but say God had not yet sufficiently scourged the City.[16]

---

[1] Studies of London in this period include W. G. Bell, *The Great Fire of London* (1920); N. Brett-James, *The Growth of Stuart London* (1935); T. F. Reddaway, *The Rebuilding of London* (1940); A. L. Beier & R. Finlay (eds), *The Making of the Metropolis: London 1500–1700* (1986).

[2] W. G. Bell, *The Great Fire of London* (1920) p 16.

[3] P. Slack, *Metropolitan Government in Crisis: the response to the Plague,* in Beier & Finlay (1986) pp 60–81 (see Note 1); W. G. Bell, *The Great Plague in London in 1665* (2nd edition 1951); P. Slack, *The Impact of Plague in Tudor & Stuart England* (1985). 'A List of Works in the Guildhall Library relating to the Plague in London, together with the Bills of Mortality 1532–1858,' in *Guildhall Miscellany* Vol II (1960–8) pp 306–317.

[4] D. Keene, *Cheapside before the Great Fire* (1985) p 20.

[5] R. Finlay & B. Shearer, *Population Growth and Suburban Expansion,* in Beier & Finlay (1986) pp 37–59 (see Note 1).

[6] J. Evelyn, *Fumifugium: or the Inconvenience of the Aer and Smoak Dissipated* (1661).

[7] For a general account of 17th century political history see J. P. Kenyon, *Stuart England* (2nd edition 1985); I Roots, *The Great Rebellion 1640–1660* (1966); for London's role in the Civil War see V. Pearl, *London and the Outbreak of the Puritan Revolution* (1961).

[8] S. Rolle, *London's Resurrection: or, the Rebuilding of London* (1668).

[9] J. Stow, *The Survey of London* (1603: Everyman Edition published 1970); for an illustrated summary of London's medieval buildings see J. Schofield, *The Buildings of London from the Conquest to the Great Fire* (1984).

[10] See Note 5.

[11] M. J. Power, *The Social Topography of Restoration London,* in Beier & Finlay (1986) pp 199–223 (see Note 1).

[12] See Note 4, pp 14–6.

[13] *Calendar State Papers Domestic 1664–5,* cxvii, 102–3.

[14] Anon, *The Compleat Parish Officer* (1738), p 38.

[15] Most of these prophecies are selected from those published by Bell in *The Great Fire of London* (1920), p 18.

[16] D. Defoe, *A Journal of the Plague Year* (1722, Penguin Edition 1966).

PART TWO:

The Fire Chronicle

'In 1666, London burned like rotten sticks'

In the following section, a comprehensive selection of the eye-witness accounts of the Fire is presented. It provides a detailed description of the events in London summarised below, from the early morning of Sunday 2nd September, 1666 when fire broke out in Pudding Lane, to Friday 7th, by which time most of the City was in ruins.

It all began, by accident or negligence, in Thomas Faryner's bakehouse. The crowded buildings in London were tinder-dry after a hot summer: the quay-side just to the south of Pudding Lane was packed with combustibles such as timber, oil and pitch. It was therefore hardly surprising that the Fire, beginning in the middle of the night, spread so quickly in its early stages before enough people were awake to the danger. With hindsight, it is easy to blame Londoners for not acting faster to get the Fire under control on the Sunday morning. Many citizens understandably refused to allow their houses to be pulled down to create adequate firebreaks: others, like Samuel Pepys, simply thought the fire a long way off and of little consequence, and went back to bed. They had seen fires in London before, and this one looked no different. Later that morning, it proved to be very different. Fanned by a driving east wind, it jumped whatever firebreaks those who were trying to fight it could create. In spite of the endeavours of the parish and ward officials, and even of the Lord Mayor, Sir Thomas Bludworth, it became obvious that the Fire was out of hand, and the firefighters efforts were ineffective. The City could not save itself.

Charles II, arriving from Whitehall to inspect the damage, could do little more. By that afternoon the Fire had destroyed all waterfront buildings almost as far west as Three Cranes (present-day Southwark Bridge), but had also begun burning northwards up the hill towards Cheapside. All attempts to create firebreaks were in vain, and Londoners began gathering up their possessions and fleeing, abandoning the City to the flames.

The Fire burnt all night, and gained momentum throughout Monday. By order of the King, the Duke of York (the future James II) was placed in control of the City, and his guards tried to keep the peace and prevent further disorder or looting. Firebreaks at Queenhithe were ineffective, and the Fire advanced west towards the Fleet River and north beyond Cornhill and the Royal Exchange. Belated arrangements were made to check the progress of the conflagration on the northern and western sides of the City with the establishment of Fire Posts, each manned by 130 men with orders to create fire breaks in a particular area. Had such a system been used earlier, much might have been saved.

By Tuesday morning, even these measures seemed inadequate, and the militia from Middlesex, Hertfordshire and Kent were ordered into the City to prevent riots and fight the Fire. Not even the Fleet River served as an effective firebreak: later that day, having destroyed St Paul's, the Guildhall and much else, the flames burst out of the City gates, leaped the Fleet and attacked Fleet Street. Now, for the first time, Whitehall and the Royal residences were threatened. In the east, gunpowder was used to clear firebreaks and save the Tower of London. This proved effective, and again, had such a tactic been introduced earlier, as the seamen had suggested, the story could well have been different.

On Tuesday night, when all seemed lost, the wind dropped and changed direction. Only then could the tired firefighters begin to check, control and dowse the flames, to which tasks they expended their efforts on Wednesday and Thursday. By Friday they had succeeded and, exhausted, could stop and begin to count the cost. The devastation which now stared out at them was horrific. London was a vast, unrecognisable blackened ruin.

SUNDAY SEPTEMBER 2nd 1666:
never was there the like Sabbath in London

11. The approximate extent of the Fire by the end of Sunday; it had been raging out of control for less than 24 hours. (C. Milne after W. Bell)

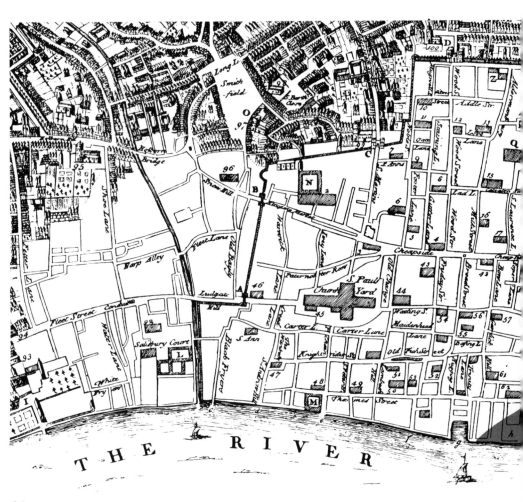

Thomas Faryner, baker of Pudding Lane, claimed that he had, after midnight on Saturday, 1st September 1666 'gone through every room [in the bakery] and found no fire, but in one chimney, where the room was paved with bricks, which fire I diligently raked up in embers . . . no window or door might let wind in to disturb them, and that it was absolutely set fire on purpose'[1]

Robert Viner:

About two in the morning [Thomas Faryner and his family] felt themselves almost choked with smoke, and rising, did find the fire coming upstairs; so they rose to save themselves; but, at that time, the bavins [faggots] were not on fire in the yard . . .[2]

London Gazette, no 85:

At one of the clock in the morning, there happened to break out a sad deplorable fire in Pudding Lane, near Fish Street Hill, which falling out at that hour of the night, and in a quarter of the town so close built with wooden pitched

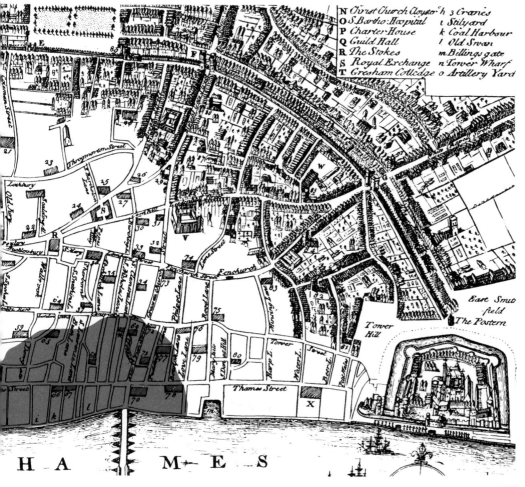

houses, spread itself so far before the day, and with such distraction to the inhabitants and neighbours, that care was not taken for the timely preventing the further diffusion of it, by pulling down houses, as ought to have been; so that this lamentable fire in a short time became too big to be mastered by any engines or working near it. It fell out most unhappily too, that a violent easterly wind fomented it, and kept it burning all that day, and the night following, spreading itself up to Gracechurch Street, and downwards from Cannon Street to the waterside as far as the Three Cranes in the Vintry.

Thomas Vincent:
The fire begins, is quickly taken notice of, though in the midst the night 'Fire! Fire! Fire!' doth resound the streets: many citizens start out of their sleep: look out of their windows; some dress themselves and run to the place.

 The Lord Mayor of the City comes with his officers: a confusion there is: council is taken away: and London, so famous for wisdom and dexterity, can now find neither brains nor hands to prevent its ruin . . .

Edward Waterhouse:
And the first circumstance notable in it is that of the time when it began which was ominous, as it was about 3 of the clock on a Sunday morning, a time when most persons, especially the poorer sort, were but newly in bed and in their first dead sleep, for Saturday being the conclusion of the week's labour, and the day of receipts and payments, the markets last not then only all the day, but the some part of the night. . . . And thence might the fire get a more then ordinary rooting, from the leisure of its burning before it met with check or supression. Yea, and when it was discovered, the usual custom being to lie longest in bed on sunday might make men more indulge their ease and remit their early stirrings and wanted vigour then otherwise they would . . .

Samuel Pepys:
Lord's Day. Some of our maids sitting up late last night to get things ready against our feast today, Jane called us up, about 3 in the morning, to tell us of a

12. A London bakehouse. *The illustration shows the type of ovens in which the Great Fire started. Note the bundle of faggots (bavins) lying on the floor next to the large bee-hive oven*

great fire they saw in the City. So I rose, and slipped on my nightgown and went to her window and thought it to be on the back side of Mark Lane at the farthest, but being unused to such fires as followed, I thought it far enough off, and so went to bed and to sleep.

Edward Waterhouse:

This pityful lane, [Pudding Lane] crowded in behind little Eastcheap . . ., St Botolph's Lane on the east, and Thames Street on the south of it was the place where the Fire originated, and that forwarded by a baker's stack of wood in the house, and by all the neighbouring houses, which were as so many matches to kindle and carry it on to its havoc.

Thus the fire meeting with the Star Inn on Fish Street Hill on the back of it, and that Inn full of hay and other combustibles, and with houses opposite to it and closed with it at the top, burned three ways at once: into Thames Street (the lodge of all combustibles, oil, hemp, flax, pitch, tar, cordage, hops, wines, brandies and other materials favourable to fire, all heavy goods being warehoused there near the waterside, and all the wharfs for coal, timber, wood etc being in a line consumed by it); unto Fish Street Hill, till it met the other fire at the bridge to the interval of building and to Botolph's Lane into Mark Lane in Tower Street, and in all this savage progress met with no opposition from engines or other artifices because it was impossible in such a street and in such a rage of fire they should be serviceable for if all the engineers of mischief would have compacted the irremediable burning of London, they could not have laid the scene of their fatal contrivance more desperately to a probable success than there where it was, where narrow streets, old buildings all of timber, all contiguous each to other, all stuffed with ailment for the fire, all in the very heart of the trade and wealth of the City.

Thomas Vincent:

But now the fire gets mastery and burns dreadfully; and God with his great bellows blows upon it, which makes it spread quickly and go on with such force and rage, overturning all so furiously that the whole City is brought into jeopardy of desolation. That night most of the Londoners had taken their last sleep in their houses; they little thought it would be so when they went into their beds; they did not in the least suspect when the doors of their ears were unlocked, and the casements of their eyes were opened in the morning, to hear of such an enemy invading the City; and that they should see him, with such fury, enter the doors of their houses, break into every room, and look out of their casements with such a threatening countenance.

Samuel Pepys:

About 7 am rose again to dress myself, and there looked out at the window and saw the fire not so much as it was, and further off. So to my closet to set things to rights after yesterday's cleaning. By and by Jane comes and tells me that she hears that above 300 houses have been burned down tonight by the fire we saw, and that it was now burning down all Fish Street Hill by London Bridge.

So I made myself ready presently, and walked to the Tower and there got

up upon one of the high places . . . and there did see the houses at that end of
the bridge all on fire, and an infinite great fire on this and the other side the
end of the bridge, which, among other people, did trouble me for poor little
Michell and our Sarah on the Bridge. So down, with my heart full of trouble,
to the Lieutenant of the Tower, who tells me that it begun this morning in the
King's baker's house in Pudding Lane, and that it hath burned down St
Magnus Church and most part of Fish Street Hill already.

So I down to the waterside and there got a boat and through the bridge, and
there saw a lamentable fire. Poor Michell's house, as far as the Old Swan,
already burned that way and the fire running further, that in a very little time
it got as far as the Steelyard while I was there. Everybody endeavouring to
remove their goods and flinging into the river or bringing them into lighters
that lay off. Poor people staying in their houses as long as till the very fire
touched them, and then running into boats or clambering from one pair of
stairs by the waterside to another. And among other things, the poor pigeons,
I perceive were loathe to leave their houses, but hovered about the windows
and balconies till they were some of them burned their wings, and fell down.

Thomas Vincent:

The beginning of the fire at such a time, when there had been so much hot
weather which had dried the houses and made them the more fit for fuel; the
beginning of it in such a place where there were so many timber houses and
the shops filled with so much combustible matter; the beginning of it just
when the wind did blow fiercely upon that corner towards the rest of the City
which then was like tinder to the sparks: this doth smell of a Popish design,
hatched in the same place where the Gunpowder plot was contrived . . .

Now the trained bands are up in arms watching at every quarter for Outlan-
dish [foreign] men because of the general fears and jealousies, and the
rumours that fire balls were thrown into houses by several of them to help on
and provoke the too furious flames.

Now goods are hastily removed from the lower parts of the City, and the
body of the people begin to retire and draw upwards.

Samuel Pepys:

Having stayed, and in an hour's time seen the fire rage every way, and
nobody to my sight endeavouring to quench it, but to remove their goods and
leave all to the fire; and having seen it get as far as the Steelyard, and the wind
mighty high and driving it into the City, and everything, after so long a
drought, proving combustible, even the very stones of churches . . . I to
Whitehall . . . and there up to the King's closet in the chapel, where people
came about me and I did given them an account which dismayed them all; and
word was carried in to the King. So I was called for and did tell the King and
Duke of York what I saw, and that unless his Majesty did command houses to
be pulled down, nothing could stop the fire. They seemed much troubled,
and the King commanded me to go to my Lord Mayor from him and
command him to spare no houses but to pull down before the fire everyway,
The Duke of York bid me tell him that if he would have any more soldiers, he
shall; and so did my Lord Arlington afterward, as a great secret.

Here meeting with Captain Cocke, I in his coach, which he lent me, and Creed with me, to St Paul's, and there walked along Watling Street as well as I could, every creature, coming away laden with goods to save – and here sick people carried away in beds. Extraordinary good goods carried in carts and on backs. At last met my Lord Mayor [Sir Thomas Bludworth] in Cannon Street, like a man spent, with a scarf about his neck. To the King's message, he cried like a fainting woman:

'Lord, what can I do? I am spent! People will not obey me. I *have* been pulling down houses. But the fire overtakes us faster than we can do it'. That he needed no more soldiers; and that for himself, he must go and refresh himself, having been up all night. So he left me, and I him, and walked home – seeing people all almost distracted and no manner of means used to quench the fire. The houses too, so very thick thereabouts, and full of matter for burning as pitch and tar, in Thames Street – and warehouses of oil and wines and brandy and other things . . .

As soon as dined, I and Moone away and walked through the City, the streets full of nothing but people and horses and carts laden with goods ready to run over one another, and removing goods from one burned house to another . . . among others I now saw my little goldsmith Stokes receiving some friend's goods, whose house itself was burned the day after. We parted at Paul's, he home and I to Paul's Wharf, where I had appointed a boat to

13. St Botolph's Lane, Billingsgate: Sunday 2nd September, 1666. *The warehouses on the Thames waterfront were full of combustible products, and so added fuel to an already ferocious fire. This photograph shows the remains of burnt-out cellars excavated in 1983. To the north, under the plastic shelter in the top left-hand corner, are the ruins of St Botolph's church, one of the 87 churches destroyed in the Fire*

These Engins (which are . . . . the best) to quinch great Fires, are

JOHN KEELING Fecit

14. John Keeling's 17th-century fire engine

attend me . . . below and above the bridge, to and again, to see the fire, which was now got further, both below and above, and no likelihood of stopping it.

Met with the King and the Duke of York in their barge, and with them to Queenhithe and there called Sir Richard Browne [an Alderman, and colonel in the City militia] to them. Their order was only to pull down houses apace, and so below bridge at the waterside, but little was or could be done, the fire coming upon them so fast. Good hopes there was of stopping it at the Three Cranes above, and at Botolphs Wharf below the bridge, if care be used. But the wind carries it into the City, so as we know not by the waterside what it doth there. River full of lighters and boats taking in goods swimming in the water; and only, I observed that hardly one lighter or boat in three that had the goods of a house in, but there was a pair of virginalls in it.

Thomas Vincent:
Yet some hopes were retained on the Lord's day that the fire would be extinguished, especially by them who lived in the remote parts: they could scarcely imagine that the fire a mile off should be able to reach their houses.

But the evening draws on and now the fire is more visible and dreadful: instead of the black curtains of the night which used to be spread over the City, now the curtains are yellow, the smoke that arose from the burning parts seemed like so much flame in the night, which being blown upon the other parts by the wind, the whole City at some distance seemed to be on fire.

Now hope begins to sink, and a general consternation seizes upon the spirits of the people: little sleep is taken in London this night: the amazement which the eye and ear doth effect upon the spirit, doth either dry up or drive

15. The Great Fire
made short work of
buildings like these
which would have been
typical of those found
in City back-streets in
1666. This particular
view is of buildings
near Grub Street still
standing in 1791.
(From John T. Smith's
Ancient
Topography of
London, 1815).

away the vapour which used to bind up the senses. Some are at work to quench the fire with water: others endeavour to stop its course by pulling down of houses, but all to no purpose: if it can be a little allayed or beaten down, or put to a stand in some places, it is but a very little while: it quickly recruits and recovers its force, it leaps, it mounts and makes the move upon the waterhouses and engines, burns them, spoils them, and makes them unfit for service. Some are on their knees in the night, pouring out their tears before the Lord, interceding for poor London in the day of its calamity, but alas . . . London's sins were too great and God's anger against the City was too hot, so easily and presently to be quenched . . .

The time of London's fall is come: the fire hath received its commission from God to burn down the City, therefore all attempts to hinder it are in vain.

John Evelyn:

After dinner, the fire continuing, with my wife and son took coach and went to the bank side in Southwark, where we beheld the dismal spectacle, the whole City in dreadful flames near the waterside, and now consumed all the houses from the bridge all Thames Street and upwards towards Cheapside, down to Three Cranes, and so returned exceedingly astonished what would become of the rest.

Samuel Pepys:

Having seen as much as I could now, I away to Whitehall . . . and there met my wife and Creed and his wife and walked to my boat, and there upon the water again, and so the fire up and down, it still increasing and the wind great. So near the fire as we could for smoke; and all over the Thames, with one's face in the wind you were almost burned with a shower of firedrops – this is very true – so as houses were burned by these drops and flakes of fire, three or four, nay five or six houses, one from another. When we could endure no more upon the water, we to a little alehouse on the Bankside over against the Three Cranes, and there stayed till it was dark almost and saw the fire grow; and as it grow darker, appeared more and more, and in corners and upon steeples and between churches and houses as far as we could see up the hill of the City, in a most horrid malicious bloody flame, not like the fine flame of an ordinary fire . . . We stayed till, it being darkish, we saw the fire as only one entire arch of fire from this to the other side the bridge, and in a bow up the hill for an arch of above a mile long. It made me weep to see it. The churches, houses, and all on fire and flaming at once, and a horrid noise the flames made, and the cracking of houses at their ruin.

So home with a sad heart . . . I did remove my money and iron chests into my cellar, as thinking that the safest place. And got my bags of gold into my office ready to carry away, and my chief papers of accounts also there, and my tallies into a box by themselves . . .

Thomas Vincent:

Never was there the like Sabbath in London: some churches were in flame that day . . . such warm preaching those churches never had: such lightening dreadful sermons never were before delivered in London. In other churches.

ministers were preaching their farewell sermons, and the people were hearing with quaking and astonishment: instead of a holy rest, which christians have taken on this day, there is a tumultuous hurrying about, the streets towards the place that burned, and more tumultuous hurrying upon the spirits of those that sat still, and had only notice of the ear, of the quick and strange spreading of the fire.

On the Lord's Day night, the fire had run as far as Garlickhithe in Thames Street, had crept up into Cannon Street and levelled it to the ground and is still making forward by the waterside, and upward to the brow of the hill, on which the City is built.

MONDAY SEPTEMBER 3rd 1666:
a Bow with Fire in it

16. Now the flames roared north, east and west across London 'like a bow with fire in it'. (C. Milne after W. Bell)

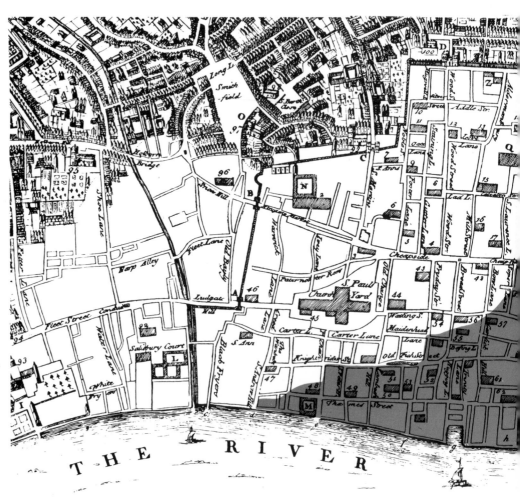

Thomas Vincent:

On Monday Gracechurch Street is all in flames, with Lombard Street on the left hand and part of Fenchurch Street on the right, the fire working (though not so fast) against the wind that way: before it were pleasant and stately houses: behind it ruinous and desolate heaps. The burning then was in the fashion of a bow, a dreadful bow it was, such as mine eyes never before had seen: a bow which had God's arrow in it with a flaming point. It was a shining bow, not like that in the cloud which brings water with it and withal signifies God's covenant not to destroy the world any more with water, but it was a bow which had fire in it, which signified God's anger and his intention to destroy London with Fire.

Now the flames break into Cornhill, that large and spacious street, and quickly cross the way by the train of wood that lay in the streets untaken away, which had been pulled down from houses to prevent its spreading: and so they lick the whole street as they go: they mount up to the top of the highest houses; they descend down to the bottom of the lowest vaults and cellars; and

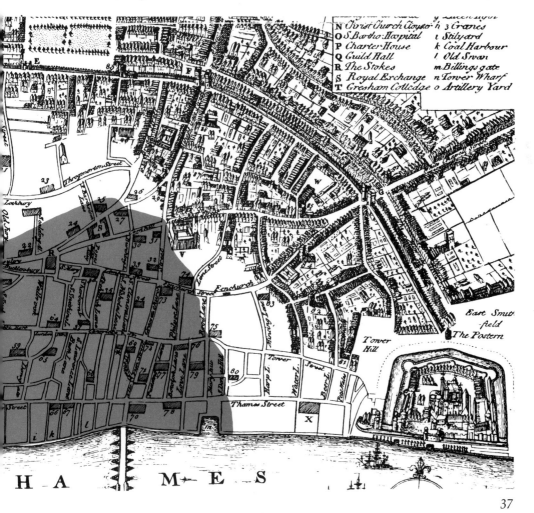

17. The Royal Exchange. *Most of the City's major civic buildings were destroyed in the Fire. The Royal Exchange, 'the glory of the merchants', met its fate on Monday, together with all the buildings and churches in the lanes clustering around it. Only one of the statues which adorned the niches around the central courtyard survived: the figure was that of Thomas Gresham, founder of the Exchange*

march along both sides of the way with such a roaring noise as never was heard in the City of London: no stately building so great as to resist their fury. The Royal Exchange itself, the glory of the merchants, is now invaded with much violence: and when once the fire was entered, how quickly did it run round the galleries, filling them with flames: then came down the stairs, compasses the walks, giving forth flaming volleys and filled the court with sheets of fire: by and by down fall all the kings upon their faces, and the greatest part of the stone building after them (the founders statue only remaining) with such noise as was dreadful and astonishing.

Then, then the City did shake indeed, and the inhabitants tremble and flew away in great amazement from their houses, lest the flames should devour them. Rattle, Rattle, Rattle was the noise which the fire struck upon the ear round about, as if there had been a thousand iron chariots beating upon the stones. And if you opened your eye to the opening of the streets where the fire was come, you might see in some places whole streets at once in flames, that issued forth, as if they had been so many great forges from the opposite windows which folding together, were united into one great flame throughout the whole street: and then you might see the house tumble, tumble, tumble from one end of the street to the other with a great crash, leaving the foundations open to the view of the heavens.

Samuel Pepys:

About 4 a-clock in the morning, my Lady Batten sent me a cart to carry away all my money and plate and best things to Sir W. Riders at Bethnal Green; which I did, riding myself in my nightgown in the cart; and Lord! to see how the streets and the highways are crowded with people, running and riding and getting of carts at any rate to fetch away things. I find Sir W. Rider tired with being called up all night and receiving things from several friends. His house full of goods, and much of Sir W. Batten's and Sir W. Penn's. I am eased at heart to have my treasure so well secured. Then home with much ado to find a way. Nor any sleep all this night to me or my poor wife . . .

Thomas Vincent:

Now fearfulness and terror doth surprise the citizens of London; confusion and astonishment doth fall upon them at this unheard of judgement. It would have grieved the heart of an unconcerned person to see the rueful look, the pale cheek, the tears trickling down from the eyes (where the greatness of

18. Cornhill in the 17th century. *The pump is at the intersection with Gracechurch Street, Bishopsgate and Leadenhall Street. The church of St Peter Upon Cornhill (right) and Leadenhall (left) are also visible. (Pub. 1814)*

sorrow and amazement could give leave for such a vent), the smiting of the breast, the wringing of the hand; to hear the sighs and groans, the doleful weeping speeches of the distressed citizens, when they were bringing forth their wives (some from their child bed) and their little ones (some from their sick bed) out of their houses and sending them into the country or some where into the fields with their goods. Now the hopes of London are gone: their heart is sunk now there is a general remove in the City and that in a greater hurry than before the Plague, their goods being in greater danger then by the Fire than their persons were by the sickness. Scarcely are some returned, but they must remove again, and not as before, now without any more hopes of ever returning and living in those houses any more.

Now carts and drays and coaches and horses as many as could have entrance into the City were loaded and any money is given for help, £5, £10, £20, £30 for cart, to bear forth into the fields some choice things, which were ready to be consumed: and some of the countrys had he conscience to accept of the highest price, which the citizens did offer in their extremity: I am mistaken if such money do not burn worse than the fire out of which it was raked.

Now casks of wine and oil and other commodities are tumbled along and the owners shove as much of their goods as they can towards the gate: every one now becomes a porter to himself, and scarcely a back either of man or woman that hath strength, but had a burden on it in the streets. It was very sad to see such throngs of poor citizens coming in and going forth from the unburnt parts, heavy laden with some pieces of their goods, but more heavy laden with weighty grief and sorrow, so that it was wonderful they did not quite sink under these burdens.

John Evelyn:
Here we saw the Thames covered with goods floating, all the barges and boats laden with what some had time and courage to save, as on the other, the carts etc carrying out to the fields which for many miles were strewed with movables of all sorts, and tents erecting to shelter both people and what goods they could get away with.

Samuel Pepys:
The Duke of York came this day by the office and spoke to us, and did ride with his guard up and down the City to keep all quiet, he being now General, and having care of all.

extract from Dutch letter:
The people believed that the Dutch and the French had set fire to the City. They said the conflagration was begun by a Dutch baker, who was bribed to do this work, and that the French went about scattering fireballs in the houses. All foreigners alike were held to be guilty, no discrimination being shown, and many who were well known to be of good character, and on whom no suspicion could rest, were cast into prison. Amongst them was the brother of Mr Germius, who has the appearance of a Frenchman, and because of that he was grossly ill-treated . . . A Dutch baker in Westminster, Riedtveldt, heated his oven to bake bread. The people, seeing smoke issuing from the chimney, cried out that the rogue was setting the town on fire at that end,

19. James II (1633–1701). *Once it became clear that the Lord Mayor and the City authorities were unable to contain the disaster, James Stuart, the then Duke of York, tried to co-ordinate the firefighters' efforts.*

and they dragged him out into the street, severerly wounding him, and they beat him nearly to death. The Duke of York happened to pass the house just in time to save the man from being murdered. The mob plundered his house, and the baker is completely ruined. One sees in the City nothing but doorways and chimneys standing amongst the ruins. It will be a long time before the people of London forget their wild rage against the foreigners.[3]

John Evelyn:
The fire having continued all this night (if I may call that night, which was as light as day for ten miles around about after a dreadful manner) when conspiring with a fierce eastern wind, in a very dry season, I went on foot to the same place when I saw the whole south part of the City burning from Cheapside to the Thames, and all along Cornhill (for it likewise kindled back against the wind as well as forward), Tower Street, Fenchurch Street, Gracechurch Street, and so along to Baynard's Castle, and was now taking hold of St Paul's Church, to which the scaffolds contributed exceedingly.

The conflagration was so universal and the people so astonished, that from the beginning (I know not by what desponding or fate) they hardly stirred to quench it, so as there was nothing heard or seen but crying out and lamentation and running about like distracted creatures, without at all attempting to save even their goods; such a strange consternation there was upon them, so as it burned both in breadth and length, the churches, public halls, Exchange,

20. The south front of Baynard's Castle c1640. *Not even the massive masonry bulk of this castle at the south-west corner of the City, could withstand the Fire; it was a burnt-out shell by Monday night*

21. The foundations of the octagonal corner tower of Baynard's Castle were excavated in 1981, and dwarf the 0.5m scale resting on its southern wall

hospitals, monuments and ornaments, leaping after a prodigious manner from house to house and street to street at great distance one from another for the heat (with a long set of fair and warm weather) had even ignited the air and prepared the materials to conceive the fire, which devoured after an incredible manner houses, furniture, and everything.

Thomas Vincent:

Monday night was a dreadful night, when the winds of the night had shadowed the light of the heavenly bodies, there was no darkness of night in London, for the fire shines now round about with a fearful blaze which yielded such a light in the streets as it had been the sun at noon day.

Now the fire having wrought backwards strangely against the wind to Billingsgate etc along Thames Street eastwards, runs up the hill to Tower Street and having marched on from Gracechurch Street, maketh further progress in Fenchurch Street, and having spread its wings beyond Queenhithe in Thames Street westwards, mounts up from the waterside through Dowgate and Old Fish Street into Watling Street.

But the great fury of the fire was in the broader streets: in the midst of the night it was come down Cornhill, and laid it in the dust, and runs along by the Stocks, and there meets another fire which came down Threadneedle Street, a little further with another which came up from Walbrook, a little further with another which comes up from Bucklersbury, and all these four joining together, break into one great flame at the corner of Cheapside with such a dazzling light and burning heat and roaring noise by the fall of so many houses together that was very amazing. And though it were something stopped in its swift course at Mercers chapel, yet with great force in a while it conquers the place and burns through it, and then with a great rage proceedeth forward in Cheapside.

Calendar of State Papers Domestic, 1666–7:

J. Hickes, senior clerk of the Post Office, reported that Sir Phillip Frowde and his lady fled from the Post Office (near the Stocks Market, Mansion House) at midnight for safety; stayed himself till 1 am, till his wife and children's patience could stay no longer, fearing least they should be quite stopped up: the passage was so tedious they had much ado to get where they are. The Chester and Irish mails have come in, but he knows not how to dispose of the business. Is sending his wife and children to Barnet (CLXX, 61).

John Evelyn:

Oh the miserable and calamitous spectacle, such as happily the whole world had not seen the like since the foundation of it, nor to be outdone, till the Universal Conflagration of it, all the sky were of a fiery aspect, like the top of a burning oven, and the light seen above forty miles round for many nights.

God grant mine eyes may never behold the like, who now saw above ten thousand homes all in one flame, the noise and crackling and thunder of the impetuous flames, the shrieking of women and children, the hurry of people, the fall of towers, houses and churches was like an hideous storm, and air all about so hot and inflamed that at last one was not able to approach it, so they

22. *Old Temple Bar which stood at the entrance to the City in Fleet Street just east of today's Law Courts*

were forced to stand still and let the flames consume on which they did for near two whole miles in length and one in breadth. The clouds also of smoke were dismal and reached upon computation near fifty miles in length.

Thus I left it this afternoon burning, a resemblance of Sodom, or the Last Day. It called to mind that of 4 Hebrews: *non enim hic habemus stabilem Civitatem*, the ruins resembling the picture of Troy: London was, but is no more. Thus I returned.

Calendar State Papers Domestic 1666–7:
Lord Arlington endorses lists of eight fire-fighting posts, at which the constables of the respective parishes are ordered to attend, each with 100 men during the Fire. At every post there are to be 30 foot soldiers with a good careful officer, 2 or 3 gentlemen who are to have power to give 1 shilling to any who are diligent all night. These men are to be relieved from the country tomorrow. £5 in bread, cheese and beer allowed to every post. Two companies of trained bands are to guard people's goods in Lincoln's Inn Fields, Gray's Inn Fields, Hatton Garden and St Giles Fields, and a good officer to go round several posts at this end of the town to see these orders executed. List of Fire Posts:-

23. This contemporary view of the Fire, painted by a Dutch artist, shows the 'burnt Londoners' fleeing eastwards past the Tower away from the flames. Those with carts for hire were charging up to £30 for their services

45

24. Old St Paul's Cathedral, west front, before the Fire. *The newly-faced west end of Old St Paul's, as it appeared to Hollar in the mid-17th century. Unfortunately it was undergoing repairs on the eve of the Fire, and so part of it was encased by timber scaffolding. The flames ran up to the roof and brought it crashing down, destroying thousands of pounds-worth of books and other goods which had been stored for safety in the vaults.*

25. A Soldier of a Trained Band, 1638. *With no standing army or police force the trained bands were the only organised forces available to keep law and order in such an emergency.*

1) Temple Bar to St Dunstan's: Lord Bellays, Mr Chichley, Mr May.
2) Clifford's Inn Gardens to Fetter Lane: Sir Chas Wheeler, Sir Godfrey Floid, Col Lowland.
3) Fetter Lane to Shoe Lane: Fran Berkley, Rich Hopton, Sir Geo Charnal.
4) Shoe Lane to Holborn Bridge: Col Whittley, Mr Arch Berkley, Mr Ed Halsall.
5) Cow Lane to Cock Lane: Sir John Taylor, Sir Robert Murray, Sir Wm Roberts.
6) Aldersgate: Sir Paul Neale, Mr Marmaduke Dasey.
7) Cripplegate and Surgeons Hall: Mr Thos Gray, Sir Ed Murray.
8) Coleman Street: Sir John Harmer, Col FitzGerald.

Sir Wm Coventry, writing to Lord Arlington, states that the Duke of York fears for the want of workmen and tools tomorrow morning and wishes the deputy lieutenants and justices of the peace to summon the workmen with tools to be there by break of day. In some churches and chapels are great hooks for pulling down houses, which should be brought ready upon the place tonight against the morning.

John Lord Berkley (at the Tower) writes to Sir Wm Batten enclosing a warrant for the delivery of all water engines remaining in store at Deptford and Woolwich, on account of the dreadful fire now raging: also for the attendance of all persons, capable either by hand or judgement, to assist in the preservation of the Tower.
(CLXX 59, 60, 65, 66, 122)

TUESDAY SEPTEMBER 4th 1666:
universal conflagration

*26. Extent of the Fire
on Tuesday and
Wednesday. (C.
Milne after W. Bell)*

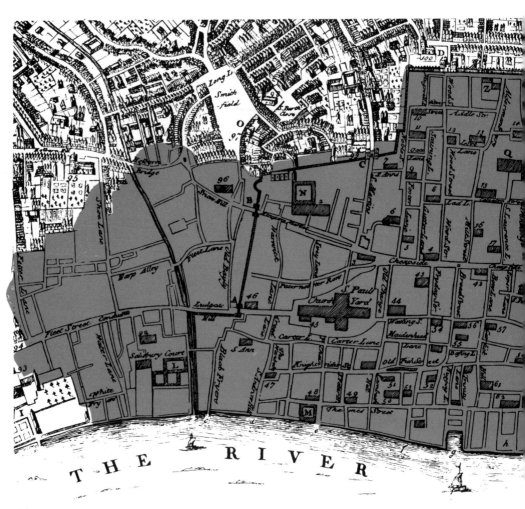

Thomas Vincent:

On Tuesday was the fire burning up the very bowels of London: Cheapside is all in a light fire in a few hours time many fires meeting there as in the centre; from Soper Lane; Bow Lane; Bread Street; Friday Street and Old Change, the fire comes up almost together and breaks furiously into Broad Street and most of that side of the way was together in flames (a dreadful spectacle!) and then partly by the fire which came down by Mercer's Chapel, partly by the fall of the houses cross the way, the other side is quickly kindled, and doth not stand long after it. Now the fire gets into Blackfriars and so continues its course by the water and makes up towards Paul's Church on that side, and the Cheapside fire besets the great building on this side, and the church, although of stone outward, though naked of houses about it, and though so high above all buildings in the City, yet within a while doth yield to the violent assaults of the conquering flames, and strangely takes the fire at the top. Now the lead melts and runs down, as if it had been snow before the sun, and the

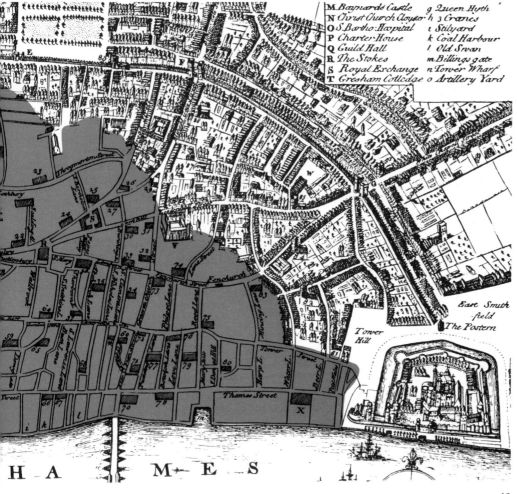

27. On Tuesday, the Fire engulfed St Paul's and half the City. This contemporary German drawing shows the flames, fanned by the east wind, marching towards Whitehall.

Opposite:
28. St Paul's before the Fire. From Visscher's Panorama of London *(1616).*

great beams and massive stones with a great noise fall on the pavement and break through into Faith's Church underneath: now great flakes of stone scale and peel off strangely from the side of the walls; the Conqueror having got this high fort, darts its flames around about, now Paternoster Row, Newgate Market, Old Bailey and Ludgate Hill have submitted themselves to the devouring fire which with wonderful speed rusheth down the hill into Fleet Street.

Now Cheapside fire marcheth along Ironmonger Lane, Milk Street, Wood Street, Gutter Lane, Foster Lane. Now it runs along Lothbury, Cateaten Street [Gresham St] etc. From Newgate Street it assaults Christchurch and conquers the great building and burns through Martin's Lane towards Aldersgate, and all about so furiously as if it would not leave a house standing upon the ground.

John Evelyn:

The burning still rages; I went on horseback and it was now gotten as far as Inner Temple; all Fleet Street, Old Bailey, Ludgate Hill, Warwick Lane, Newgate, Pauls Chain, Watling Street now flaming and most of it reduced to ashes, the stones of St Pauls flew like grenades, the lead melting down the streets in a stream, and the very pavements of them glowing with fiery redness, so as nor horse nor man was able to tread on them, and the demolitions had stopped all the passages so as no help could be applied; the eastern wind still more impetuously driving the flames forwards. Nothing but the almighty

S PAULES CHURCH

THAMESIS

The Eall Schipes

Three Cranes

The Gally fufte

Etiam periere Ruinæ

W. Hollar fecit. A° 1666

29. The Burning of St Paul's. Engraving by Wencelaus Hollar.

Opposite: 30. St Mary Aldermary, Bow Lane. The church standing in 1666 was begun in 1510, but only the tower survived the Fire. Funds bequeathed for its rebuilding stipulated that it was to be rebuilt in its original style, and Wren's gothic design, shown here, complied with that request.

power of God was able to stop them, for vain was the help of man.

London Gazette, no 85

The people in all parts about it distracted by the vastness of it, and their particular care to carry away their goods, many attempts were made to prevent the spreading of it by pulling down houses, and making great intervals, but all in vain, the fire seizing upon the timber and the rubbish and so continuing itself, even through those spaces, and raging in a bright flame all Monday and Tuesday, notwithstanding His Majesties own and the Duke of York's indefatigable and personal pains to apply all possible remedies to prevent it, calling upon and helping the people with their guards; and a great number of nobility and gentry unweariedly assisting therein.

Calendar State Papers Domestic 1666–7):

Warrant for removing the Exchequer to Nonsuch, Surrey: majors, bailiffs etc to assist therein, at their peril. (CLXX, 93)

Wind. Sandys:

Being constant with the Duke of York I presume to believe none have seen more of it than I have, he being so active and stirring in this business, he being all the day long from five in the morning till eleven or twelve at night, using all means possible to save the rest of the City and the suburbs. On Tuesday our only hope was to save Fleet Street, and so to Whitehall, by pulling down

The Parish Church of St. Mary Aldermary in Bow Lane.

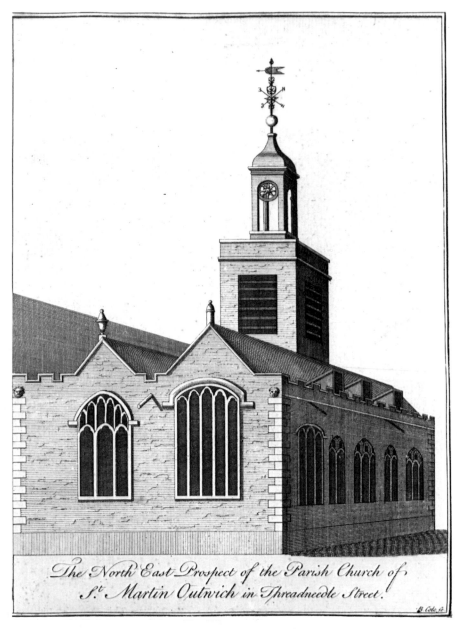

The North East Prospect of the Parish Church of
S.ᵗ Martin Outwich in Threadneedle Street.

31. St Martin
Outwich,
Threadneedle
Street, *in 1756. This
church survived the
Great Fire, only to be
burnt down in 1765.
Its successor was
demolished in 1874.*

houses both sides of Bridewell Dock [the Fleet River] so to make a broad lane
up from the River [Thames] to Holborn Bridge. The Duke's [station] was from
Fleet Bridge to the river; Lord Craven . . . was to come from Holborn Bridge
to Fleet Bridge; the Privy Council to assist him with powder, there being a law
among the citizens that whoever pulleth down a house shall build it up again,
so what was done was by order of the King and Council.

All orders signified nothing; had not the Duke been present and forced all
people to submit to his orders, by this time I am confident there had not been a

house standing near Whitehall. The City, for the first rank, they minded only for their own preservation; the people of the middle sort so distracted and amazed that they did not know what they did; the poorer, they minded nothing but pilfering; and so the City abandoned to the fire and thousands believing in Mother Shipton's prophecy 'that London in '66 should be burnt to ashes' . . . a judgment upon the City for their former sins.

The Duke on Tuesday, about twelve o'clock, was environed with fire; the wind high, blowed such great flakes, and so far, that they fired Salisbury Court and several of the houses between that and Bridewell Dock, so that the duke was forced to fly for it, and had almost been stifled with the heat. The next hope there was to stop it at Somerset House, it raged so extreme in Fleet Street on both sides and got between us, and at six of the clock to the King's Bench Office at the Temple. Night coming on, the flames increased by the wind rising, which appeared to us so terrible to see, from the very ditch the shore quite up to the Temple all in flame, and a very great breadth. At ten o'clock at night we left Somerset House, where they had begun to pull down some houses in hopes to save Whitehall, by pulling down Sir John Denham's

32. The Fire burnt its way down Ludgate Hill and burst through Ludgate, shown here with St Paul's blazing in the background. Then the flames leapt the Fleet River to the west of the City and began attacking the suburbs. Now even the King's palace at Whitehall was threatened

33. South View of the Custom House of London, in the reign of Queen Elizabeth. *The Fire also made progress eastwards into the prevailing wind. The Custom House in which Geoffrey Chaucer had worked 300 years earlier was gutted on the Thursday*

buildings, and so up to Charing Cross. The Queen and Duchess resolved to be gone by six o'clock on Wednesday morning to Hampton Court. Nothing can be like unto the distraction we were in, but the Day of Judgment.[4]

Samuel Pepys:

Up by break of day to get away the remainder of my things, which I did by a lighter at the Irongate Stairs; and my hands so few, that it was the afternoon before we could get them all away.

Sir W. Penn and I to Tower Street, and there met the fire burning three or four doors beyond Mr Howell's, whose goods, trays and dishes, shovels etc were flung all along Tower Street in the drainage gutters, and people working therewith from one end to the other, the fire coming on in that narrow street on both sides with infinite fury. Sir W. Batten, not knowing how to remove his wine, did dig a pit in the garden and laid it in there; and I took the opportunity of laying all the papers of my office that I could not otherwise dispose of. And in the evening Sir W. Penn and I did dig another, and I my Parmazan cheese as well as my wine and some other things.

34. *Within the City, timber buildings like these had no protection from the flames of 1666. This particular building on the corner of Fleet Street and Chancery Lane outside the City survived the Fire, but was demolished in 1859.*

Thomas Vincent:

Now horrible flakes of fire mount up into the sky and the yellow smoke of London ascendeth up the heaven like the smoke of a great furnace; a smoke so great, as darkened the sun at noon-day (if at any time the sun peeped forth, it looked red like blood) the cloud of smoke was so great that travellers did ride at noon-day some miles together in the smoke thereof, though there were no other clouds beside to be seen in the sky.

Samuel Pepys:
This afternoon, sitting melancholy with Sir W. Penn in our garden and thinking of the certain burning of this office without extraordinary means, I did propose for the sending up of all our workmen from Woolwich and Deptford yards (none whereof yet appeared), and to write to Sir W. Coventry to have the Duke of York's permission to pull down houses rather than lose this office, which would much hinder the King's business. So Sir W. Penn went down this night, in order to the sending them up tomorrow morning, and I wrote to Sir W. Coventry about the business, but received no answer.

That night Mrs Turner . . . and her husband supped with my wife and I . . . in the office upon a shoulder of mutton from the cook's, without any napkin or anything. in a sad manner, but were merry. Only now and then walking into the garden and saw how horribly the sky looks, all on a fire in the night was enough to put us out of our wits; and indeed it was extremely dreadful – for it looks just as if it was at us, and the whole heaven on fire. I after supper walked in the dark down to Tower Street, and there saw it all on fire at the Trinity House on that side and the Dolphin Tavern on this side, which was very near us – and the fire with extraordinary vehemence.

Now begins the practice of blowing up houses in Tower Street, those next to the Tower, which at first did frighten people more than anything. But it stopped the fire where it was done, it bringing down the houses to the ground in the same places they stood, and then it was easy to quench what little fire was in it, though it kindled nothing almost.

W. Hewer this day went to see how his mother did, and comes late home, but telling us how he hath been forced to remove her to Islington, her house in Pye Corner being burned. So that it is got so far that way and all the Old Bailey, and was running down to Fleet Street. And St Paul's is burned, and all Cheapside. I wrote to my father this night, but the post-house being burned, the letter could not go.

Calendar State Papers Domestic 1666–7:
Lord Arlington, writing to Sir Thomas Clifford:
God has visited the City with a heavy calamity. . . . A fire has burned . . . with such a violence that no art or pain can meddle with it . . . I leave you to judge what a distraction this misfortune put us into, whereof the consequences are yet more terrible to us, by the disorders that are likely to follow. For these considerations, His Majesty by the unanimous concurrence of his council, wishes my Lord General [the Duke of Albemarle] were here [he was with the English Fleet about to attack the Dutch] . . . If my Lord General could see the condition we are in, I am confident and so is everybody else, he would think it more an honour to be called to this occasion . . . [where] it is certain he will have it in his hands to give the King his kingdoms a second time. (CLXX, 93)

Calendar State Papers Domestic 1666–7:
Charles II writes to the Lord Lieutenants of Middlesex, Surrey and Hertfordshire. Since the hand of God is laid on the City by a raging fire, he enjoins

them for the prevention of unhappy consequences in the disturbance of peace and quiet, to draw together the militia of those counties at the most fitting rendezvous, giving timely notice of all that occurs (CLXX, 94).

Thomas Vincent:

And if Monday night was dreadful, Tuesday night was more dreadful, when the greatest part of the City was consumed: many thousands who on Saturday had houses convenient in the City both for themselves and to entertain others, now have not where to lay their heads, and the Fields are the only receptacle which they can find for themselves and their goods: most of the late inhabitants of London lie all night in the open air with no other canopy over them, but that of the heavens. The fire is still making towards them, and threatens the suburbs: it was amazing to see how it had spread itself several miles in compass and amongst other things that night, the sight of the Guildhall was a fearful spectacle, which stood the whole body of it together in view, for several hours together after the fire had taken it without flames (I suppose because the timber was such solid oak) in a bright shining coal as if it had been a palace of gold or a great building of burnished brass.

WEDNESDAY SEPTEMBER 5th 1666:
the Court bestirs itself

Samuel Pepys:
I lay down in the office again . . . being mighty weary and sore in my feet with going till I was hardly able to stand. About 2 in the morning my wife calls up and tells of new cries of 'Fire!', it being come to All Hallows Barking church, which is the bottom of our lane. I up, and finding it so resolved presently to take her away; and did, and took my gold, which was about £2,350, W. Hewer and Jane down by Proundy's boat to Woolwich. But Lord! what a sad sight it was by moonlight to see the whole City almost on fire – that you might see it plain at Woolwich, as if you were by it. There when I came, I find the dock-yard gates shut, but no guard kept at all; which troubled me, because of discourses now begun that there is plot in it and that the French had done it. I got the gates open, and to Mr Sheldon's, where I locked up my gold and charged my wife and Mr Hewer never to leave the room without one of them in it night or day. So back again, by the way seeing my goods well in the light-ers at Deptford and watched well by people.

Thomas Vincent:
On Wednesday morning when many people expected that the suburbs would be burnt as well as the City and with speed were preparing their flight as well as they could with their luggage into the countrys and neighbouring villages. Then the Lord hath pity on poor London: his bowels begin to relent, his heart is turned within him, and he stays his rough wind in the day of the east wind: his fury begins to be allayed; he hath a remnant of people in London and there shall a remnant of houses escape: the wind is now hushed: the commission of the fire is now withdrawing, and it burns so gently, even when it meets with no opposition that it is not hard to be quenched, in many places with few hands: now the citizens begin to gather a little heart and encouragement in their endeavours to quench the fire.

John Evelyn:
On the 5th it crossed towards Whitehall but Oh the confusion was then at

court. It pleased his Majesty to command me among the rest to look after the quenching of Fetter Lane end, to preserve (if possible) that part of Holborn, whilst the rest of the Gentlemen took their several posts, some at one part, some at another for now they began to bestir themselves, and not till now, who had stood as men interdict, with their hands a crosse, and began to consider that nothing was like to put a stop, but the blowing up of so many houses as might make a wider gap than any had yet been made by the ordinary method of pulling them down with engines. This some stout seamen proposed early enough to have saved the whole City, but some tenacious and avaricious men, aldermen etc would not permit because their house must have been the first. It was therefore now commanded to be practised and my concern being particularly for the Hospital of St Bartholomews near Smithfield, where I had many wounded and sick men, made me the the more diligent to promote it: not was my care for the Savoy less.

Wind. Sandys:

About eleven o'clock on Tuesday night came several messengers to the Duke [of York] for help, and for engines, and said that there was some hopes of stopping it; that the wind was got to the south, and had blown the fire upon those houses from the street between the side of the Temple Church; by that means had took off the great rage of the fire at that side, and on the side of the street St Dunstan's Church gave a check to it. We had not this mercy shown to us alone, but likewise hearts and hands from the people; the soldiers being almost all tired out with continual labour. By six o'clock on Wednesday morning the Duke was there again, and found the fire almost quenched on both sides of the street; from thence he went to the Rolls, caused all people, men, women, and children that were able to work to come, and to those who refused he beat them to it; by this means he got people to other places, as Fetter Lane, which he preserved by the assistance of some brick houses and garden walls; likewise Shoe Lane . . . At Holborn Bridge there was my Lord Craven, who gave a check to the fire there, and by noon quenched it. It then broke out again in Cow Lane in Smithfield; so Lord Craven went to assist Sir Richard Brown who is but a weak man in this business. The Lord Mayor went to Cripplegate, pulled down a great store of houses there to stop it, being grown to a great head. The Lords of the Privy Council ride about to every place, to get pipes opened that they may not want water, as the Lord Chamberlain, Lord Ashley and others, so that by Wednesday towards the evening we supposed the fire everywhere quenched excepting that about Cripplegate, which we hoped well of.[4]

Extract from account printed in Padua, Italy:

On Wednesday . . . another fire, having reduced the Exchange to ashes, spread north, consuming everything on its way up to Moorfields, where the King, the Duke of York, and all the nobles came to see King Charles I avenged. But moved to pity by the terrible spectacle, they gave themselves an example to the citizens by throwing buckets of water on the fire, exhorting the populace to do the same. The people, who had saved such part of their goods

DRAWN AND ETCHED BY J.T.SMITH.   SACRED ARCHITECTURE.   DRAWN IN JUNE 1812
NORTH-EAST VIEW OF PARTS OF THE CHAPEL AND GRANARY OF LEADENHALL.
Pubᵈ Octoʳ 1ᵗ 1815, by J.T. Smith, Nº 18, Gᵗ May's Buildings, Sᵗ Martins Lane.

35. A view of the chapel and granary within the Leadenhall complex. *Although these medieval buildings were some of the few which survived the Fire, they did not survive 19th-century redevelopments*

as they had been able to lay hands on, and neglected what was now past recovery, began, on the King's instigation, to work manfully, and soon the fire was extinguished in that part of the City also.[5]

Henry Griffiths:

All stood to the mercy of an enraged fire which did . . . almost destroy the metropolis of this Isle, had not God of his infinite mercy stayed the fury thereof, which was done by his Majesty's and the Duke of York's singular care and pains, handing the water in buckets when they stood up to the ankles in water, and playing the engines for many hours together, as they did at the Temple and Cripplegate, which people seeing, fell to work with effect, having so good fellow labourers.[6]

John Evelyn:

So as it pleased Almighty God by abating of the wind and the industry of people. now when all was lost, infusing a new spirit into them (and such as had exerted in time undoubtedly preserved the whole) that the fury of it

36. 'A check it had at Leadenhall': *the progress of the Fire was arrested by the massive masonry buildings of Leadenhall in the east of the City. This is part of the west face which defied the flames on the Wednesday, discovered and recorded over 300 years later. (10 × 100mm scale)*

began sensibly to abate about noon, so as it came no further than the Temple westwards, not the entrance of Smithfield north, but continued all this day and night so impetuous toward Cripplegate and the Tower, as made us even all despair. It also broke out again in the Temple, but the courage of the multitude persisting, and innumerable houses blown up with gunpowder, such gaps and desolations were soon made, as also by the former three days consumption as the back fire did so vehemently urge upon the rest, as formerly.

Thomas Vincent:

A check it had at Leadenhall by that great building: a stop it had in Bishopsgate, Fenchurch Street, Lime Street, Mark Lane and towards the Tower: one means, under God, was the blowing up of houses with gunpowder. Now it is stayed in Lothbury, Broad Street, Coleman Street; towards the gates it burnt, but not with any great violence: at the Temple also it stayed, and at Holborn, where it had no great footing: when once the fire was got under, it was kept under, and on Thursday the flames were extinguished.

John Evelyn:

There was yet no standing near the burning and glowing ruins near a furlong's space; the coal and wood wharfs and magazines of oil, rosin etc did infinite mischief, so as the invective I but little before dedicated to his Majesty and published, giving warning in the City, was looked on as prophetic.

But there I left this smoking and sultry heap, which mounted up in dismal clouds night and day, the poor inhabitants dispersed all about St Georges, Moorfields, as far as Highgate and several miles in circle, some under tents others under miserable huts and hovels without a rag or any necessary utensils, bed or board who from delicateness, riches and easy accommodations in stately and well furnished houses were now reduced to extremest misery and poverty.

In this calamitous condition I returned with a sad heart to my house, blessing and adoring the distinguishing mercy of God to me and mine who in the midst of all this ruin was like Lot in my little Zoar, safe and sound.

Calendar State Papers Domestic 1666–7:

Charles II writes to Griffth Bourda, to inform him that a very great number of distressed persons from London have taken refuge with their goods which they have with difficulty saved from the Fire in the houses and fields about Islington. However, they are in danger of being deprived of what they have, since there are no deputy lieutenants and justices of the peace in that parish. Requests that strict watch may be kept in all the ways within the limits of that town and parish, and that charitable and christian reception, lodging and entertainment be given to the strangers. Commands all inhabitants to obey orders for keeping watch and ward (CLXX, 95).

Proclamation ordering that, for the supply of the distressed people left destitute by the late dreadful and dismal Fire, the King has ordered great proportions of bread to be brought daily not only to the former markets, but to those lately ordained; that all churches, chapels, schools and public buildings are to be kept open to receive the goods of those who know not how to

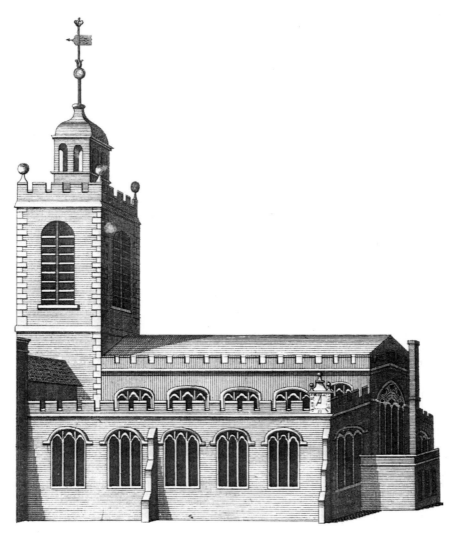

37. All Hallows
Barking. *This church,*
now usually called All
Hallows by the Tower,
survived the Fire. Its
new brick tower built
in 1659 during the
Cromwellian period
foreshadowed some of
Wren's later church
designs.

dispose of them; that other towns receive the said distressed persons and
permit them to exercise their trades, on promise that they shall afterwards be
no burden to them (CLXX, 96).

Samuel Pepys:
Home, and whereas I expected to have seen our house on fire, it being now
about 7 o'clock, it was not.

But to the fire, and there find greater hopes than I expected; for my confi-
dence of finding our office on fire was such that I durst not ask anybody how it
was with us, till I came and saw it not burned. But going to the fire, I find, by
the blowing up of houses and the great help given by the workmen out of the
King's Yards sent up by Sir W. Penn, there is a good stop given to it, as well as

38. The Great Fire was extinguished to the west of the City just before it reached the ancient Temple Church.

at Mark Lane end as ours – it having only burned the dial of Allhallows Barking church, and part of the porch, and was there quenched.

I up to the top of the steeple, and there saw the saddest sight of desolation I ever saw; everywhere great fires, oil-cellars and brimstone and other things burning. I became afeared to stay there long, and therefore down again as fast as I could, the fire being spread as far I could see it, and to Sir W. Penn's and there eat a piece of cold meat, having eaten nothing since Sunday but the remains of Sunday's dinner . . . having removed all my things and received good hopes that the fire at our end is stopped, . . . I walked into the town and find Fenchurch Street, Gracechurch Street and Lombard Street all in dust. The Exchange a sad sight, nothing standing there of all the statues or pillars but Sir Thomas Gresham's picture in the corner. Walked into Moorfields (our feet ready to burn, walking through the town among red hot coals) and find that full of people and poor wretches carrying their goods there, and everybody keeping his goods together by themselves (and a great blessing it is fair weather for them to keep abroad night and day); drank there, and paid two pence for a plain penny loaf.

Thence homeward having passed through Cheapside and Newgate market, all burned, and seen Anthony Joyce's house on fire. And took up (which keep by me) a piece of glass of Mercer's chapel in the street, where much more was, so melted and buckled with the heat of the fire, like parchment. I also did see a poor cat taken out of a hole in the chimney joining the Exchange, with the hair all burned off the body and yet alive. So home at night, and find good good hopes of saving our office – but great endeavours of watching all night and have men ready; and so we lodged them in the office, and had drink and bread and cheese for them.

Thomas Vincent:

But on Wednesday night, when the people late of London, now of the Fields, hoped to get a little rest on the ground where they had spread their beds, a more dreadful fear falls upon them than they had before, through a rumour that the French were coming armed against them to cut their throats and spoil them of what they saved out of the fire . . . yet many citizens having lost their houses and almost all they had are fired with rage and fury and they begin to stir up themselves like lions or like bears bereaved of their whelps and now 'Arm! Arm! Arm!' doth resound the Fields and suburbs with a dreadful voice. We may guess at the distress and perplexity of the people this night which was something alleviated when the falseness of the alarm was perceived.

Samuel Pepys:

And I lay down and slept a good night about midnight, though when I rose, I hear that there had been a great alarm of French and Dutch being risen, which proved nothing. But it is a strange thing to see how long this time did look since Sunday, having been always full of variety of actions, and little sleep, that it looked like a week or more. And I forgot almost the day of the week.

THURSDAY SEPTEMBER 6th 1666: extinguishing the flame

Earl of Oxford, reporting upon his round of the Fire Posts:

My Lord Chamberlain, Dr Ashley and Lord Hollis were not found at Ely House;

at *Temple Bar* all the constables appointed to attend were wanting, as also the Lord Bellayse and Mr May. Mr Chicheley was upon the place;

At *Clifford's Inn* all the constables were also absent, but upon the post were found Sir Charles Wheeler, Sir Godfrey Floid, Col Lowdan;

Fetter Lane all the constables likewise wanting, as also Mr Rich Hopton, Sir Geo Charnall. Mr Fran Berkley upon the place;

Holborn Bridge was attended by constables, as also there present Col Whitely, Mr Arch Barklay, Mr Edw Halsal;

Cow Lane and Cock Lane were not attended by the constables, but upon the place were Sir John Sayers, Sir Wm Roberts, but not Sir Robert Murray;

At *Aldersgate* was upon the place Sir Marmaduke Darsey, Sir Paul Neale absent;

Cripplegate and Surgeons Hall were found nobody;

Coleman Street were upon the place Sir John Harmor, Sir Allen Apsley; Col FitzGerald.

In all these places I found places where the fire had been well-watched with sentinels and all care possible used by them that were present. Major Miller's whole company stood at Holborn bridge, persistently very vigilant and constantly moving between that place and Smithfield, he deserves encouragement. This is mine own hand, Oxford.[7]

Calendar State Papers Domestic 1666–7:

Lord Ashley Cooper sends list of names of seamen who had done good service in stopping the Fire ever since Sunday to Charles II (CLXX 124).

Lord Arlington, writing to the Lord Lieutenant of Hertfordshire, tells him that he warned on September 4th to draw the militia troops together for service of the City; the raging fire is now abated, but all hands being wearied

39. The old Merchant Taylors' Hall in Threadneedle Street. The building was gutted but the shell survived the Fire

with working, 200 foot soldiers are to be marched thither with food for 48 hours, and carts laden with pick axes, ropes and buckets etc to prevent the further spreading of the Fire. They are to rendezvous at Kingsland, near Bishopsgate, and the justices of peace and deputy lieutenants are to be assembled, to quicken them in the execution of orders, and also to forward the bringing in of provisions, especially bread and cheese, into the City, lest the want thereof add to the calamity (CLXX, 126).

John Evelyn:

I represented to his Majesty the case of the French prisoners of war in my custody and besought him there might be still the same care of watching at all places contiguous to unseized houses.

It is not indeed imaginable how extraordinary the vigilance and activity of the King and Duke was, even labouring in person and being present to command, order, reward and encourage workmen; by which he shewed his affection to his people and gained theirs.

Overleaf:
40. A prospect of London after the Fire. From an engraving by Wenceslaus Hollar, 1666. The gaunt shells of masonry buildings rise above acres of smouldering debris as far as the eye can see

A TRVE AND EXACT PROSPECT OF THE FAMOVS

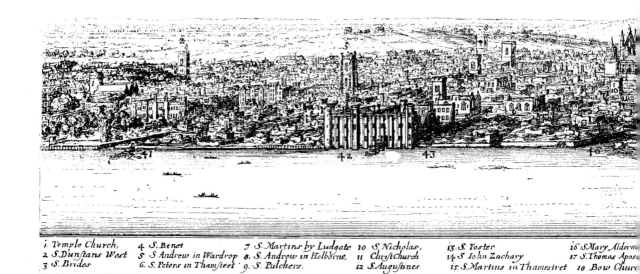

1. Temple Church,	4 S. Benet	7 S. Martins by Ludgate	10 S. Nicholas,	13. S. Foster	16 S. Mary Aldern
2 S. Dunstans West	5 S Andrew in Wardrop	8. S. Andrew in Holborne,	11 Christ Church	14 S. Iohn Zachary	17 S. Thomas Apos
3 S. Brides	6. S. Peters in Thamstreet	9. S. Pulchers.	12 S. Augustines	15 S. Martins in Thamestreet	18 Bow Churc

APPEARETH NOW AFTER THE SAD CALAMITIE AN

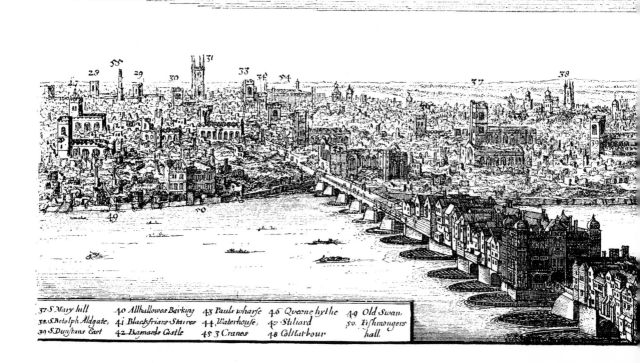

37 S. Mary hill	40 Allhallowes Barking	43 Pauls wharfe	46 Queene hythe	49 Old Swan,
38. S. Botolph Aldgate,	41 Blackfriars Staires	44 Waterhouse,	47 Stiliard	50. Fishmongers
39 S. Dunstans East	42 Baynards Castle	45 3 Cranes	48 Colltarbour	hall.

	22. Allhallowes y'creat	25. S. Mary Wolnoth	28. S. Christopher	31. S. Michael Cornhill	34. S. Denis.
S. Laurence	23. S. Stevens Colman stret	26. S. Lorence Poultney	29. S. Bartholomew	32. Allhallowes	35. S. Magnus.
S. Mary Buttolf lane	24. S. Margaret.	27. S. Stevens in Walbroke,	30. S. Edmunds,	33. S. Peters in Cornhill,	36. S. Andrew Hubart

DESTRVCTION BY FIRE, In the Yeare. M.DC.LXVI.

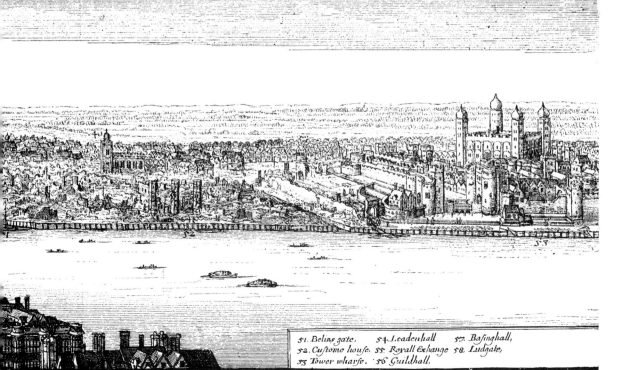

51. Belins gate,	54. Leadenhall	57. Basinghall,
52. Custome house,	55. Royall Exchange	58. Ludgate,
53. Tower wharfe,	56. Guildhall,	

Wenceslaus Hollar: delin: et sculp: 1666,

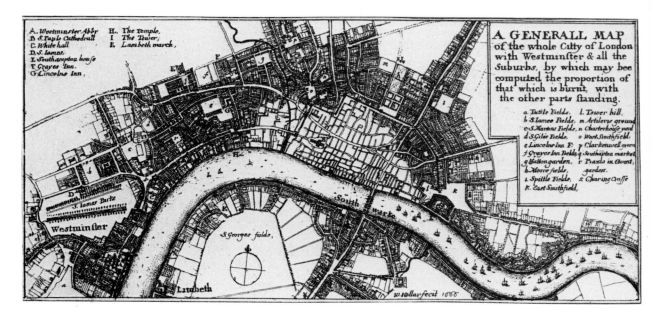

A. Westminster Abby
B. S Pauls Cathedrall
C. White hall
D. S. James
E. Southampton house
F. Grayes Inn
G. Lincolns Inn

H. The Temple,
I. The Tower,
K. Lambeth march,

A GENERALL MAP
of the whole Citty of London
with Westminster & all the
Suburbs, by which may bee
computed the proportion of
that which is burnt, with
the other parts standing.

a. Tuttle Fields
b. S James Fields
c. S Martins Fields
d. S Giles fields
e. Lincolns Inn F.
f. Grayes Inn fields
g. Hatton garden
h. Moore fields
i. Spittle Fields
k. East Smithfield

l. Tower hill
m. Artilerie ground
n. Charterhouse yard
o. West Smithfield
p. Clarkenwell green
q. Southapton market
r. Piazza in Covent garden
s. Charing Crosse

41. Map of London and its suburbs, 1666, drawn by Wenceslaus Hollar, showing the proportion of the town destroyed in the Fire

Samuel Pepys:

Up about 5 o'clock to call our men to Bishopsgate, where no fire had yet been near, and there is now one broke out, which did give great grounds to people, and to me too, to think that there is some kind of plot in this. But I went with the men and we did put it out in a little time, so that that was well again. It was pretty to see how hard the women did work in the drainage channels sweeping of water; but then they would scold for drink and be as drunk as devils.

Calendar State Papers Domestic:

Proclamation ordering that, as the old markets are burned down, markets will be held at Bishopsgate Street, Tower Hill, Smithfield and Leadenhall, which will be well protected; and ordering the magistrates in counties whence provisions are sent to London to forward supplies. Also forbidding men to disquiet themselves with rumours of tumults, but attend the business of quenching the Fire, troops being provided to keep the peace. Also ordering Gresham College to be used instead of the Royal Exchange (CLXX, 125).

Samuel Pepys:

And now all being pretty well, I took boat and over to Southwark, and took boat on the other side the bridge and so to Westminster, thinking to shift myself, being all in dirt from top to bottom. But there could not find any place to buy a shirt or pair of gloves, Westminster Hall being full of people's goods, and the Exchequer money put into vessels to carry to Nonsuch Palace (Epsom) . . .

A sad sight to see how the river looks, no houses nor church near it to the Temple, where [the fire] stopped. To the office and there slept, with the office full of labourers, who talked and slept and walked all night long there. But strange it was to see Clothworkers Hall on fire these three days and night in one body of flame, it being the cellar full of oil.

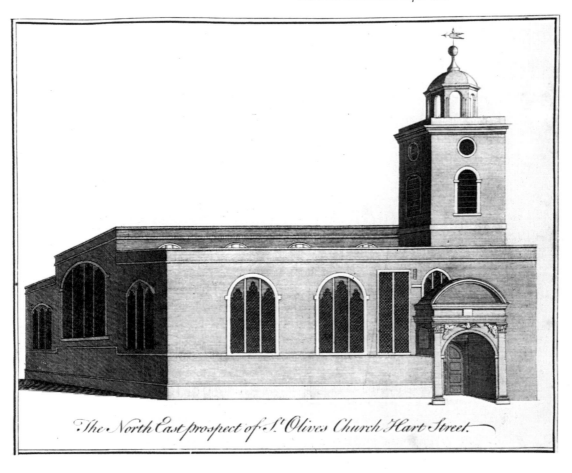

The North East prospect of S.t Olives Church Hart Street.

William Taswell

Near the walls of St Pauls, a human body presented itself to me, parched as it were with flames, whole as to the skin, meagre as to flesh, yellow as to colour. This was an old decrepit woman who had fled there for safety, imagining the flames would not have reached her there. Her clothes were burnt, and every limb reduced to a coal.[8]

Thomas Vincent:

Thus fell great London, that ancient City! that populous City! which was the Queen city of the land, and as famous as most cities in the world. . . . And yet how is London departed like smoke and her glory laid to dust?

42. St Olave's, Hart Street, where Samuel Pepys worshipped. The Fire was contained in the east of the City just before it reached this building.

FRIDAY SEPTEMBER 7th 1666:
all well

Samuel Pepys:
Up by 5 o'clock, and blessed by God! find all well, and by water to Paul's Wharf. Walked thence and saw all the town burned, and a miserable sight of Paul's church, with all the roofs fallen and the body of the quire fallen into St Faiths. St Paul's School also, Ludgate, Fleet Street, my Father's house, and the church and a good part of the Temple the like. So to Creed's lodging near the New Exchange . . . there borrowed a shirt of him, and washed . . . thence to the Swan and there drank; and so home and find all well.

John Evelyn:
When in the midst of all this calamity and confusion there was (I know not how) an Alarm begun, that the French and the Dutch (with whom we were now in hostility) were not only landed, but even entering the City, there being in truth great suspicion some days before, of those two nations joining and even now, that they had been the occasion of firing the town.

I went this morning on foot from Whitehall as far as London Bridge, through the late Fleet Street, Ludgate Hill by St Pauls, Cheapside, Exchange, Bishopsgate, Aldersgate and out to Moorfields, thence through Cornhill etc with extraordinary difficulty, clambering over mountains of yet smoking rubbish, and frequently mistaking where I was, the ground under my feet so hot, as made not only sweat, but even burnt the soles of my shoes, and put me all over in sweat.

In the meantime his Majesty got to the Tower by water to demolish the houses . . . built entirely around it, had they taken fire and attacked the White Tower where the magazines of powder lay, would undoubtedly have not only beaten down and destroyed all the bridge, but sunk and torne all the vessels in the river. . . .

At my return I was infinitely concerned to find that goodly Church St Pauls now in sad ruin, and that beautiful portico . . . (comparable to any in Europe as not long before repaired by the late King) now rent in pieces, flakes of vast stone split in sunder and nothing remaining entire but the inscription in the architrave which shewing by whom it was built (Inigo Jones), had but one letter of it defaced: which I could not but take notice of. It was astonishing to see what immense stones the heat had in a manner calcined, so as all the ornaments, columns, freezes, capitals and projectures of massive Portland stone flew off, even to the very roof, where a sheet of lead covering no less than 6 acres by measure, being totally melted. The ruins of the vaulted roof falling broke into St Faiths, (in the crypt of St Paul's) which being filled with . . . books belonging to the Stationers and carried thither for safety, they were all consumed, burning for a week. . . . It is also observable that the head over the altar at the East end was untouched, and among the divers monuments, the body of one bishop (Robert de Braybroke, Bishop of London in 1381) remained entire.

Thus lay in ashes that most venerable church, one of the ancientist pieces of early piety in the Christian world, beside near 100 more: the lead, ironwork, bells, plate etc melted, the sumptuous Exchange, the august fabric of Christ church, all the rest of the company halls, sumptuous buildings, arches, entries, all in dust. The fountains dried up and ruined whilst the very waters remained boiling. The Voragos of subterranean cellars wells and dungeons, formerly warehouses, still burning in stench and dark clouds of smoke like hell, so as in five or six miles traversing about, I did not see one load of timber unconsumed, nor many stones but what were calcined white as snow, so as the people who now walked about the ruins appeared like men in some dismal desert, or rather in some great City laid waste by an impetuous and cruel enemy, to which was added the stench that came from some poor creatures' bodies, beds and other combustible goods.

Sir Thomas Gresham's statue, though fallen to the ground from its niche in the Royal Exchange remained entire, when all those of the Kings since the Conquest were broken to pieces. Also the Water Standard in Cornhill and Queen Elizabeths effigies, with some arms on Ludgate continued with but little detriment, whilst the vast iron chains of the City streets, vast hinges, bars and gates of prisons were many of them melted and reduced to cinders by the vehement heats.

Nor was I yet able to pass through any of the narrower streets, but kept the widest, the ground and air, smoke and fiery vapour, continued so intense, my hair being almost singed and my feet unsufferably surbated. The bylanes and narrower streets were quite filled up with rubbish, nor could one have possibly known where he was, but by the ruins of some church or hall, that had some remarkable tower or pinnacle remaining.

Calendar State Papers Domestic 1666–7:

Charles II writes to the Lord lieutenants of Middlesex, Hertfordshire and Kent, reminding them that on September 4th the county militia were drawn together in case of accident arising from the Fire, and 200 foot soldiers were ordered to assist in extinguishing it. As the Fire is now over, the troops may retire, with thanks for their concurrence. Requests them still to furnish the City with tools formerly specified, and such quantities of food as they can (CLXX, 127).

43. Bridewell Palace at the entrance to the Fleet River in 1660, before it was burned in the Fire.

John Evelyn:

I then went towards Islington, and Highgate where one might have seen two hundred thousand people of all ranks and degrees, dispersed and laying along by their heaps of what they could save from the fire, deploring their loss and though ready to perish for hunger and destitution, yet not asking one penny for relief, which to me appeared a stranger sight than any I had yet beheld. His Majesty and Council indeed took all imaginable care for their relief, by Proclamation, for the Country to come in and refresh them with provisions.

Calendar State Papers Domestic 1666–7:

Lord Arlington signs a warrant for the apprehension of Thos Gaddesby, wheelwright of Islington, for using approbious words to those gentlemen who, in the late exigency, were appointed by special warrant (for want of magistrates), to keep watch and ward, to keep the peace, and to induce the inhabitants to give what christian relief and reception they could to those who took present refuge there (CLXXI, 42).

Thomas Vincent:

Now nettles are growing, owls are screeching; thieves and cut-throats are lurking. A sad face there is now in the ruinous part of London: and terrible hath the voice of the Lord been, which hath been crying, yea roaring in the City, by these dreadful judgments of the Plague and Fire, which he hath brought upon us.

THE COST OF THE FIRE

All in all, it has been calculated that the City lost 13,200 houses, St Paul's Cathedral, 87 parish churches, 6 consecrated chapels, the Guildhall, the Royal Exchange, the Custom House, Sessions House, 52 Company Halls, Blackwell Hall, Bridewell, Newgate Gaol, the Wood Street and Poultry Compters, 3 City gates, 4 stone bridges, at least £2,000,000-worth of printed books and paper in shops and warehouses, and £1,500,000-worth of wine, tobacco, sugar, plums etc 'of which the City was at that time very full'. A total loss amounting to some £10,000,000 is indicated, at a time when the City of London's annual income was *c* £12,000.

But what was the cost in human lives? Unfortunately, it is not possible to know how many died as a direct result of the disaster, since the weekly Bills of Mortality of the two weeks commencing 29th August 1666 do not seem to have been compiled, as was the usual practice. This is hardly surprising in the circumstances given the dangers and disruptions of the time. Working in temporary accommodation since their hall had been destroyed, the Parish Clerks were able to publish figures for the week commencing 25th September 1666. These show that 266 people died from a variety of causes in that particular week. Since this is a lower figure than that for the week before the Fire, it cannot represent three weeks fatalities. It therefore appears that there is no surviving record of the burials during the Fire period. Even the General Bill for Mortality for all of 1666 does not have a special category for deaths caused specifically by the Fire, although it does include 43 killed by several accidents, and 10 found dead in streets and fields.[9]

All that can be said is that it is known that some people died in the Fire, as John Evelyn and William Taswell witnessed, but the figure cannot have been large, or it would presumably have been recorded in some way: the 1,998 people who died of the Plague in 1666 were all counted, as were the 68,596 who suffered the same fate the previous year. How many homeless people died of cold in the harsh winter that followed the Fire is also not known.

One of the few recorded deaths indirectly attributable to the Fire is that of poor Robert Hubert, the confused Frenchman who actually confessed to starting the blaze in the bakehouse. He was tried and found guilty, even though nobody believed his story, which was inconsistent and obviously untrue. Nevertheless, Thomas Faryner, the baker, was quick to add his signature to the death warrant to take the blame off his shoulders. The young Frenchman was executed in October 1666, three months before the official Parliamentary enquiry decided that the Fire was started accidentally. Presumably Mr Faryner had not raked all his embers as diligently as he might have on the fated Saturday night.

The contemporary accounts of the Fire published here include T. Vincent, *God's Terrible Voice in the City* (1667); E. Waterhouse, *A short Narrative of the late dreadful Fire* (1667); (both these rare volumes are in the Guildhall Library, London); *The Diary of Samuel Pepys, Vol V, July 1665–Sept 30th 1666*, edited by H. Wheatley (1904); *The Diary of John Evelyn, Vol III, 1650–72* edited by E de Beer (1955); and the *Calendar of State Papers Domestic 1666–7*. See also '*A select list of printed works relating to the Great Fire of 1666 and the Rebuilding of London*, in *Guildhall Miscellany* Vol II (1960–8), pp 369–376.

[1] October Sessions at the Old Bailey, London (1666).
[2] H. Wheatley (ed), *The Diary of Samuel Pepys, Vol VI* (1904), 24 Feb 1667.
[3] W. G. Bell, *The Great Fire of London* (1920), p 320.
[4] *Ibid*, pp 316–7.
[5] *Ibid*, p 322.
[6] *Ibid*, pp 313–4.
[7] Public Records Office, SP 29/1/170/123; this document was transcribed by Alison Blake.
[8] G. P. Elliott (ed), *Autobiography and Anecdotes by Wm Taswell D.D., 1651–82* Camden Society (Old Series) *Camden Miscellany*, Vol II (1853).
[9] Parish Clerks Company, *Bills of Mortality* (1661–71).

PART THREE:

The Great Rebuilding

The Phoenix Rises

On Saturday September 1st 1666, London with its crowded late-medieval timber buildings was basking in the sun at the end of a long hot summer. Five days later it had been devastated, not, according to the Parliamentary enquiry, as a result of a Papist Plot, but . . . 'by the hand of God upon us, a great wind and the season being so very dry'.[1] However, after the Great Fire came the Great Rebuilding: five years later a substantial proportion of the City had been rebuilt. By this time many of its streets were lined with new brick buildings presenting as elegant a facade to the 18th century as any town in Europe. The Fire was therefore a mixed blessing. It not only destroyed many remarkable medieval buildings but also the equally ancient insanitary conditions which harboured the Plague and similar scourges. The town which developed in the 1670s and 1680s was cleaner and safer, the streets were wider and the buildings were more uniform, a neat well-ordered city of red brick and white stone.

It is still just possible to trace the extent of this redevelopment in the 20th century streets of London, in spite of the ravages of the Blitz and post-war urban renewal. In so doing, the negative image of the Great Fire itself is revealed. This can be seen in the illustration which shows not only the location of the churches rebuilt to Wren's designs, but also the medieval churches which lay beyond the reach of the Fire, and still survive today. Thus anyone wishing to discover for themselves the physical extent of the fire damage need only walk the circuit shown on that drawing, guided by Wren's spires and towers. This walk would be some two miles from the Tower to the Barbican and the Temple, and a further 1¼ miles back to the Tower. All of the 436-acre area enclosed within that circuit was totally devastated in September 1666, presenting the 17th century Londoners with a seemingly impossible challenge: indeed, some thought the City would never be rebuilt.

Although the physical and logistical problems of replacing 13,000 houses were daunting enough, nothing could sensibly begin before a clear plan for the City was formulated. The new plan would have to reconcile any general improvements to the City – perhaps involving major changes in its plan and

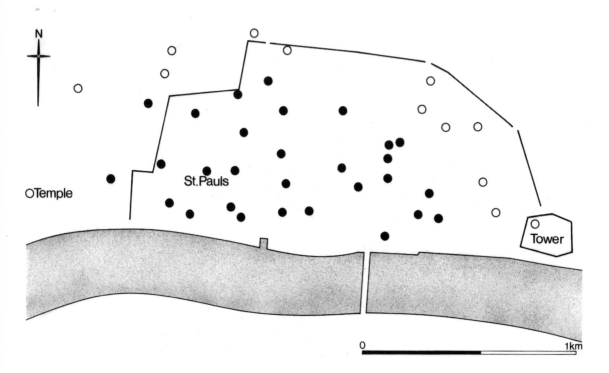

N

OTemple

St.Pauls

Tower

0   1km

44. *The imprint of the Great Fire can still be traced today, over 300 years later, as this plan of churches in the area of the walled City shows. The open circles mark the position of churches which survived the fire and which still retain some of their medieval features. They enclose the vast area from the Temple to the Tower which was devastated by the Fire, but was later occupied by the churches designed by Wren, represented here by black dots. (C. Milne)*

Opposite:
45. *Designs for a new London street plan, such as these drawn up by John Evelyn and Christopher Wren, were rejected by the City as unworkable in the autumn of 1666*

fabric – with the rights of all the individual property holders concerned. In addition, it had to be put into operation with all possible speed, for the commercial life of the City could not be conducted in temporary accommodation for an indefinite period. The business which had been so forcibly driven out of the City might never return.

There were many who had long thought that London was an ill-planned, inelegant and insanitary City: in the aftermath of the Fire, they saw an unparalleled opportunity to build a radically-new town. The proposals so promptly submitted by such men as John Evelyn, Christopher Wren, Robert Hooke, Peter Mills, Richard Newcourt and Captain Valentine Knight envisaged street plans which were markedly at variance with the cluttered medieval pattern. The speed of their submission shows that they incorporated ideas which had already been aired before the Fire. However, T. F. Reddaway has shown that these superficially-attractive schemes were prepared too hastily on inaccurate ground plans, and would therefore have required much modification before they could have been implemented.

These bold ventures were duly considered, but ultimately rejected by the City in favour of a more practical plan. The solution, adopted evolved over the autumn of 1666, and was as imaginative as it was pragmatic. It was generally agreed that the superstructue of the new City should not be a direct replication of the old. Timber building would therefore be banned in favour of brick: the old streets and lanes would be paved and widened, and

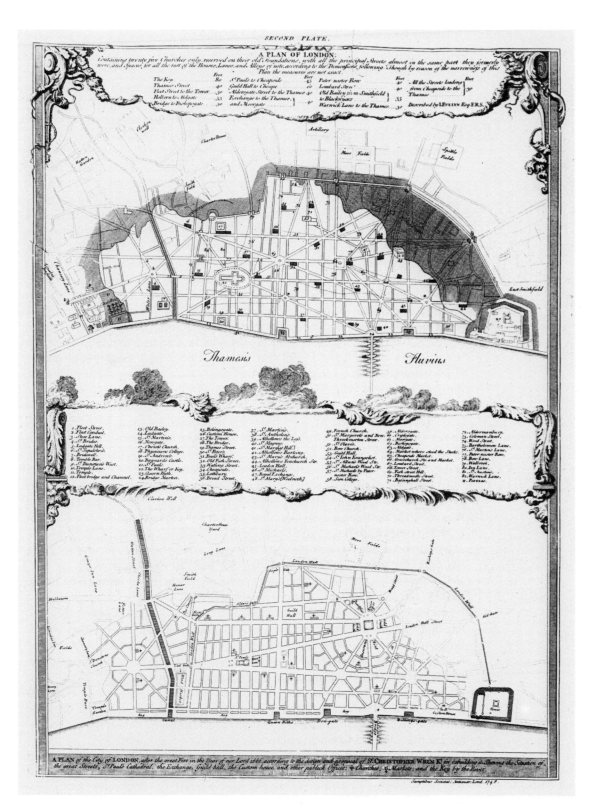

obstructions such as market buildings and conduits would be moved out of the roadways. These improvements were all to be welcomed, and the scale of the project could not be considered modest or short-sighted. The new town was to be built on the old plan, but with hygiene and access much improved, the risk of major fire decreased, and without major dislocation to the complex pattern of property ownership. It was thought that the majority of the work would take at least seven years to complete (a remarkably accurate estimate), and the workmen engaged on the rebuilding would enjoy the same privileges as Freemen of the City for that period.

The design and details of the new plan were the responsibility of six men, three royal appointments and three appointed by the City. His Majesty's Commissioners for Rebuilding were Dr Christopher Wren, better known in 1666 as the Savilian Professor of Astronomy rather than as an architect; Hugh May, the Paymaster of Works responsible for royal buildings since the Restoration, and Roger Pratt, a well-known practising architect who had studied extensively on the continent. For the City there was Robert Hooke, the distinguished scientist; Edward Jarman (later replaced by John Oliver) and Peter Mills, all of whom had considerable practical experience of all types of building in the City. Together they worked on the building regulations, house types, plans for the Fleet Canal and Thames Quay, and the street improvements ultimately embodied in the Rebuilding Act of 1667 (see Appendix 1). A number of streets were designated as major thoroughfares and were to be substantially widened, steep gradients diminished, and most of the lesser lanes were to be made at least fourteen feet wide. In total, just under 150 streets, lanes and alleys were widened, and a new north-south highway running from the Guildhall to the river stairs and ferry at Three Cranes (the present-day King and Queen Streets) was planned.

To the west of the City, the Fleet River was to be cleaned up, canalised and provided with smart wharves. The indented, irregular Thames frontage itself was to be straightened by reclaiming land at the expense of the river, and it was also proposed that a broad open space would be created on the quayside at a uniform level. To facilitate the fighting of any future waterfront fires, the building line was to be set back some forty feet from the quay wall.

The majority of the new buildings throughout the town were to be brick, build to rigidly-enforced standards. This idea had been put forward in a Commonwealth Act of 1657 which as unfortunately made void after the Restoration of 1660. It re-emerged in a more comprehensive form in the Rebuilding Act of 1667, in which it was proposed that buildings on by-streets or lanes were to be two-storied; those fronting streets and lanes of note or overlooking the Thames were to be three-storied, while merchants' mansion houses 'of the greatest bigness' and those fronting high and principal streets were to be no more than four-storied. This was to be the fabric of the new London, replacing the medieval mix of irregular, jettied buildings encroaching on narrow streets, so characteristic of the pre-Fire town.

The City had managed its finances well during the Commonwealth period in the 1650s, but it had incurred heavy expenses during the Restoration and was considerably in debt in the 1660s. As a result of the Fire, it had lost many

Monument of LONDON in remembrance of the dreadfull Fire in 1666.
Its Height is 202 feet. Printed for John Bowles at the Black Horse in Cornhill.

Collone de LONDRES elevé pour une Perpetuelle Resouvenance
Generalle de cette Ville en 1666, En Haut 202 Pied.

of its assets, and much of its income had been derived from renting out properties which were now in ruins. It was finally decided that a tax on coal could provide some of the necessary funds for rebuilding, and the Act of 1667 suggested a rate of one shilling per chaldron which came into force in June of that year. However, this proved to be inadequate, and the rate was increased to two shillings in May 1670, and three shillings in June 1677. Of the £736,000 raised in this way up to 1688, the City spent half on its public building programme (the streets, Guildhall, prisons, Fleet Canal etc). £265,000 was used to rebuild the parish churchs, and the remaining £88,000 went towards the cost of St Paul's Cathedral. By contrast, the private building programme was not assisted from these funds. The rebuilding of London was therefore the culmination of several public and private building programmes which, although chronologically and financially separate, were all part of the same centrally-planned grand design.

No work could begin on the ground until this master-plan had been completed and sanctioned by Parliament, which it was in February 1667. Then, in March, the new road pattern was staked out and the long process of infilling that huge framework could commence. Before each new house was built, the owners had to clear their foundations of debris, contact the City Suveyors and arrange for them to survey the new foundation, for which a fee of 6 shillings and eight pence was payable. The plot by plot surveys compiled by Peter Mills

46. The Monument of London in remembrance of the dreadfull Fire in 1666. *(Publ. 1751). London was elegantly rebuilt with brick buildings lining the widened streets. This is Fish Street Hill, the main road leading down to London Bridge, past the Monument*

83

47. St Vedast, Foster Lane. *One of the first churches designed by Wren to be completed after the Fire.*

and John Oliver from 1667–73 were kept by the authorities and have now been published.[2]

Sometimes, when the foundation was being set out, it became clear that the newly-staked out road cut off part of the original property, the proposed roads being wider than many of the pre-Fire lanes. In such a case, the surveyors furnished the house-owners with a certificate stating the size of the area lost, for which the City would ultimately pay compensation. There were some cases in which Londoners actually moved the staked out road-lines by dead of night in order to increase the size of their property. This was a punishable offence, but they had to be caught first. Again, on more than one occasion, houses which blatantly encroached over the agreed road line were erected. For example, the infamous Mr Selby of Mincing Lane built a block of four houses between 3 and 5ft into the street. After considerable litigation, the offending frontage was taken down by the City workmen and ultimately rectified.

Building proceeded as and when each property was ready, rather than street by street. In other words, isolated properties were often erected, 'standing so scatteringly' as Samuel Rolle described them, but with brick toothings

48. Christopher Wren (1632–1723). *Wren, one of the Commissioners for the Rebuilding of London, worked on the design of many projects, including the Fleet Canal, St Paul's Cathedral, the City churches and the New Quay*

left on both ends of the party walls so that neighbouring properties could subsequently be joined to them.

Initially, progress was slow. By the end of 1667, one year after the Fire, only 150 new buildings had been completed. This was hardly surprising, for quite apart from the vast problems of establishing a viable plan for the rebuilding, the City had had to battle through a severe winter as well as a blockade of the River Thames by a warring Dutch fleet. Thereafter the rebuilding began in earnest with some 8,000 buildings appearing in the next five years. However, by the end of 1672, c.960 sites were still open, and, more surprisingly, 3,500 of the new buildings were still unoccupied. Many of the original inhabitants had found alternative accommodation by this date, and would not return to the City. Their place was taken by the army of migrant workers and craftsmen who came originally to rebuild the town, and then settled there. Although by the end of 1673 work had begun on 500 more new dwellings, thereafter the emphasis was on the restoration of the City's churches and on St Paul's Cathedral.

The situation in 1676 is depicted on Ogilby and Morgan's famous map (published in January 1677). The majority of private houses are shown newly erected, although some vacant plots are still visible, as for example, on Brooks Wharf and Brickhill Lane, off Thames Street. However, the survival of such documents as the list of merchants and bankers compiled in 1677[3] shows that business had returned to much of the City by that date. The sites of those churches upon which work had not yet begun are simply shown as open spaces, in contrast to those churches which had been completed or at least half-built. St Paul's is shown under construction, without its roof or its main western stair.

The civic building programme began briskly with the Guildhall, the Sessions House, Custom House and Royal Exchange all completed in 1671, and the prisons were finished the following year. Work on the Fleet Canal lasted from 1671–4, and owed much to Thomas Fitch, while the Monument, thought to be designed by Robert Hooke, took three years longer.

The rebuilding of the 51 parish churches was spread over a 25 year period from 1670–95, with the majority built after 1677, ie. after the main thrust of the civic building programme was complete. Christopher Wren is credited with the design of all of these churches, but he was assisted by a large and talented team, including the young Nicholas Hawksmoor. The masons for the churches included Edward Strong, Christopher Kempster and Joshua Marshall, who all worked on St Paul's, the last of the great rebuilding schemes.

On May 1st 1666, before the Fire, Wren wrote a report on the defects of Old St Paul's and suggested that a dome might replace the crossing tower. Estimates were ordered on August 27th, but before work could begin, the Fire destroyed much of the gothic building. However, the shell was patched up and services were held in part of it until 1673, when the decision was taken to rebuild St Paul's completely, rather than just to restore it. The fate of the Norman minster was sealed. Wren had been working on a new design for St Paul's since 1670, but it was not until May 1675 that his plans received the

Royal Warrant. Work for an army of labourers and craftsmen began the next month with the laying of the foundation stone on 21st June, and continued for 35 years. The chief masons were Joshua Marshall and Thomas Strong, with Edward Strong, Christopher and William Kempster and the chief stone and wood carvers included Grinling Gibbons, Edward Pearce and Jonathan Maine. The interior plasterwork was by Henry Dougard and Chryston Wilkins, with ironwork by Tijou. Over 50,000 tons of stone from Portland, 25,000 tons from Oxfordshire, Devon, Surrey and Rutland, and 20,000 tons from Kent were needed, together with marble from Ireland, Wales, Torbay and Purbeck.

Although St Paul's was consecrated in 1697, its massive profile was still incomplete: work on the great dome and the western towers did not begin until the early years of the 18th century. The Cathedral was not pronounced finished until 1711, 45 years after the Great Fire had destroyed the old Norman minster. By this time, many of those who had lived through the Fire such as John Evelyn, Charles II, Samuel Pepys, had died, as had many who had been directly concerned with the rebuilding, such as John Oliver, Edward Jerman, Hugh May and Peter Mills. A new generation had grown up for whom those events were as distant as World War II is to us today: the late dreadful Fire was already becoming less of a memory and more of a myth or legend.

The new London incorporated town-planning on a scale that it had never

49. St Paul's Cathedral. By the turn of the 18th century St Paul's was still incomplete, and surrounded by scaffolding. This drawing shows how far Wren's design had advanced 35 years after the Fire, in 1700. Londoners had still not seen the now familiar dome and west towers. (C. Milne, from an 18th-century etching)

seen before. The scheme was revolutionary and wide-ranging, but was not so rigid that it could not be adapted whenever occasion demanded. It was not a grand fantasy from an architect's drawing board: it was a proud city's practical response to an unprecedented disaster. Nevertheless, there is still a commonly-held view that the replanning of London after the Great Fire was 'a wasted opportunity'. For example, Sir Nicholas Pevsner, the distinguished architectural historian, dismissed the adopted plan of post-Fire London as '. . . narrow, confused and medieval . . . *hardly anything was done* . . . the only new streets were Queen Street and King Street . . . All the rest was individual rebuilding on the old congested sites'.[4] This assessment is as unfair as it is inaccurate, as anything other than the briefest appraisal of the Rebuilding Act of 1667 shows (see Appendix 1). True, proposed plans for geometric street patterns slavishly reminiscent of Louis XIV's Paris were rejected by the City. This was because they were totally impractical in the circumstances, since it would have been necessary to pool all private property in the town and then distribute it equally around the new plan once complete. Some idea of just how unworkable such proposals would have been may be deduced from a study of the long sittings of the Fire Court in its offices at Cliffords Inn, Fleet Street. It took nine years deliberating on the complexities of property ownership relating to Londoners rebuilding on the *same* pre-Fire sites. The legal problems of reallocating sites on a radically different street system would clearly have delayed reconstruction and forced up the costs of compensation prohibitively.

Londoners in the 1680s were, in fact conscious of remarkable changes and certainly would not have said that '. . . hardly anything was done'. Their town had not just been substantially rebuilt with speed, care and skill: the medieval plan had been transformed into an elegant modern city of red brick and white stone. This new townscape was described in glowing terms by John Woodward MD, Gresham Lecturer in physics, in a letter to Sir Christopher Wren. '. . . So many thousand houses, of even private citizens, built in such a manner as to render them not only more convenient . . . but even superior in design and architecture to the palaces of princes elsewhere . . . Then, which I and everybody must observe with great satisfaction, by means of the enlargement of the streets, of the great plenty of good water conveyed to all parts, of the common sewers and other like contrivances, such provision is made for a free access and passage of air, for sweetness, for cleanliness, and for salubrity, that it is not only the finest, but the most healthy City in the world'.[5]

From 1550 to 1650, London grew at a faster rate than other European capitals. The population in great cities such as Amsterdam, Naples and Paris was actually declining by 1670: only in London did it continue to rise. By 1700 London had become the largest town in northern Europe: by 1750 it had even outstripped Constantinople.[6] One reason for this sustained growth could be attributed to the Fire, or, more specifically, the vast rebuilding programme. From 1667, an army of migrant workers poured into London where there was guaranteed building work at wages some 50 per cent higher than elsewhere in southern England. However, the 'burnt Londoners' not only needed 9,000 new homes, but also new furniture, new clothes, new household utensils. Such a large market obviously attracted tradesmen and craftsmen in quantity and they settled in the City and in its expanding suburbs which rapidly spread out over the former fields. The developments around Red Lion Square, Seven Dials, Soho Square and Old Bond Street all date from this period, for example. It is therefore argued that, although the Great Fire destroyed the City in 1666, the Great Rebuilding gave the expansion of London even greater impetus.

The Great Rebuilding Today:
Traces of the city which was planned and built after the Great Fire still survive, although 19th century development and the Blitz have taken a heavy toll. Some of the surviving late 17th century features have been moved and are outside London. Wren's Temple Bar (which marked the City boundary in Fleet Street) was dismantled in 1878 and re-erected in Theobald's Park, Hertfordshire, while the elaborately-carved Portland stone facade for Mercers' Hall in Cheapside was transported back to Dorset in the 19th century. It was incorporated in Swanage Town Hall in 1883, where it survives to this day unlike the rest of Mercers' Hall, which was destroyed in the Blitz. The bombing also damaged the church of St Mary Aldermanbury, but the surviving fragments were shipped to the United States of America and were re-erected in Westminster College, Fulton, Missouri. Within the ancient City of London, the best-preserved element is the street pattern itself, which, with the exception of such roads as London Wall, Queen Victoria Street, and King William Street, is in most essentials that shown on the maps of 1677. In fact some of the smaller lanes are still the same width, building line to building line, as was stipulated in the Rebuilding Acts.

Unfortunately most of the late 17th and early 18th century buildings which once lined all of these streets have been destroyed, although thirty of the churches designed by Wren survive in some form (see Appendix 2). Other buildings in the City which contain evidence of post-Fire rebuilding (but often much restored) include Apothecaries' Hall, the College of Arms, Innholders Hall, Skinners' Hall, Stationers' Hall, Tallow Chandlers' Hall, Vinters' Hall, the School House in Foster Lane, St Paul's Deanery, St Paul's Chapter House, 1–3 Amen Court, 20–22 College Hill, 1–2 Laurence Pountney Hill, 7a–9 Laurence Pountney Lane, 6 Martin Lane, 3–5 Wardrobe Place, and 79–81 Carter Lane. Off Fleet Street is Dr Johnson's House in Gough Square, and 3–5 Raquet Court. There is a considerable concentration of late 17th to early 18th century buildings near the Temple, in New Square, Middle Temple Lane, New Court, Pump Court, and Essex Court, although not all of these were direct replacements of damage caused by the Great Fire itself.

For many people, the most enduring moment to the Great Rebuilding remains St Paul's Cathedral, the City's most famous landmark. But those who are prepared to turn off the beaten track will find that the other buildings dating back to that remarkable period repay discovery.

Diary of Redevelopment

1666: THE CITY UNLIKELY TO BE BUILT AGAIN?
Sept 10:
John Evelyn: I went again to the ruins, for it was now no longer a City . . .
Sept 13:
Proclamation: general fast and collection for the burnt Londoners declared for 10 October.
Evelyn: . . . on the 13th I presented His Majesty with a survey of the ruins and a plot for a new City, with a discourse on it.
Sept 25:
Committee appointed to enquire into the cause of the Fire.
Oct 4:
Mr Hooke, reader of mathematics in Gresham College, whose exquisite model and draft for rebuilding the City prepared upon the motion and encouragement of the Common Council had received the good acceptance and approbation of that council, was appointed . . . with Mills and Edward Jermyn, to join with Dr Wren, Hugh May esq, and Sir Roger Prat appointed by the Privy Council, to make a general survey of the streets, lanes, alleys, houses and places destroyed in the Great Fire.[7]
Oct 10: **Fast Day for the Fire**
Lord Mayor orders that Londoners should clear their foundations to enable a survey to be made.
Evelyn: This day was indicated a GENERAL FAST through the nation, to humble us, upon the late dreadful conflagration, added to the Plague and War, the most dismal judgements could be inflicted and indeed but what we highly deserved for our prodigious ingratitude, burning lusts, disolute Court, profane and abominable lives, under such dispensations of God's continued favour in restoring Church, Prince and people from our late calamaties, of which we were altogether unmindful even to astonishment: this made me resolve to go to our Parish Assembly, where our Doctor preached on 19 Luke,

REceived the 26th day of *November* 1666 of Mr *Thomas Lintott* returned from *Cowfold* in *Sussex* the Summe of *fifty three shillings & Nine pence* which was collected in the said Parifh on the Faft Day, being the 10th day of *October* 1666. towards the Relief of thofe Perfons who have been great Sufferers by the late Sad Fire within the City of *London*. I fay Rec:t by order of the Lord Mayor.

Sa: Kendall.

41, ['. . . and when he was come near he beheld the city, and wept over it'] piously applying it to the occasion, after which followed a collection for the poor distressed Londoners in the late Fire, and their present relief . . .

Samuel Pepys: Up with Sir Batten by water to Whitehall . . . Thence with him to Westminster to the parish church there . . . so full, no standing, so he and I to eat herring at the Dog Tavern. And then to church again . . . and so to the Swan and basai la fille and drank and then . . . to Islington, where I find mine host dead. Here, eat drink and merry.

Oct 29:

The new Lord Mayor was sworn in at the Exchequer bar . . .; all the companies were excused attendance, except those of the two Lord Mayors and two sheriffs, who went to and from Westminster in coaches.

Pepys: . . . to see how meanly they now look, who upon this day used to be all little lords, is a sad sight . . . And everybody did reflect with pity upon that poor City . . . compared with what it heretofore was.

Robert Hubert, a Frenchman, having openly confessed to starting the Great Fire, was tried at the Old Bailey and executed at Tyburn.

Lord Clarendon: He was only accused upon his own confession; yet neither the judge nor any present at the trial did believe him guilty, but that he was a poor distracted wretch, weary of this life and chose to part with it in this way.

The signatures on the bill against Hubert include Thomas Faryner (the baker of Pudding Lane), his wife and their son.

50. The 10th October 1666 was declared a national Fast Day, and collections were made all over the country to help the 'burnt Londoners'. This receipt marks the contributions collected in Cowfold, a small village in Sussex. In 1671 it was decreed that September 2nd 'be yearly for ever after observed as a day of public fasting and humiliation within the City . . . to divert the like calamity for the time to come'

Nov 5:

Pepys: After dinner . . . I took coach . . . and find my Lord Hitchingbrook and Mr Crew and the Doctor going to see the ruins of the City . . . but Lord, what pretty and sober observations he made of the City and its desolation . . . I took them upon Tower Hill to show them what houses were pulled down since the Fire, and thence to my house, where I treated them with good wine of several sorts.

Nov 9:

Pepys ; . . . going to the dance again came news that Whitehall was on fire: and presently more particular, that the Horse Guards was on fire. And so we ran up to the garret and find it so, a horrid great fire, and by and by we saw and heard part of it blown up with powder.

Nov 22:

Pepys: My Lord Brounker did show me Hollar's new print of the City with a pretty representation of that part which is burnt, very fine indeed.

Nov 20–Dec 5:

Streets cleared of debris.

Nov 25:

Pepys: I spoke with Mr May, who tells me that the design of building the City does go on apace, and by his description it will be mighty handsome and to the satisfaction of the people: but I pray God it come out not too late.

Dec 12:

James Hicks: There are many people found murdered and carried into the vaults amongst the ruins, as three last night . . . hasty fellows cry 'do you want light' and carry links, and that when they catch a man single, whip into a vault with him, knock him down, strip him . . . and leave the persons for dead . . . For want of good watches no person dare, after the close of evening, pass the streets amongst the ruins.[8]

Dec 24:

Pepys: I walked (it being frost and dry) as far as Paul's and so back again, through the City by Guildhall, observing the ruins thereabouts, till I did truly lose myself.

Dec 31:

Pepys: Thus ends this year of public wonder and mischief to this nation; and therefore generally wished by all people to have an end. Our enemies, French and Dutch, great, and grow more by our poverty . . . The City less and less likely to be built again, everybody settling elsewhere, and nobody encouraged to trade.

1667–71: THE CITY REVIVES
1667
Feb 8:

Two bills brought before Parliament. One established the Fire Court, the other contained detailed measures concerning the actual rebuilding of London (see Appendix 1).

Feb 16:

Charles II recommends Thomas Neville, comptroller of Petty Customs in London, to be the collector of the duty of twelve pence a chaldron of coals, the proceeds of which will finance the rebuilding programmes.

Feb 27:

Draft proposals for the new lines of the streets ready.

March 5:

Hooke, Mills and Jarman to provide stakes for laying out the new streets.

March 13:

Court of Common Council appoints Mills, Jarman, Hooke and Oliver as surveyors to stake out the streets.

March 22:

Mills sets out his first foundation.

March 29:

Pepys: In my way do observe the great streets in the City are marked out with piles driven into the ground and if ever it be built in that form with so fair streets, it will be a noble sight.

April 29:

Court of Common Council prepares orders concerning the street-widening programme.

May 28:

Sir William Dugdale: There is little done as yet towards the new building of the City; all is lying in rubbish and ashes. When we look back upon the transcendent wickedness thereof, it is not to be wondered at.

June 11:

Evelyn: the Dutch, who were fallen on our fleet at Chatham, by a most audacious enterprise entering the very river with part of their fleet doing us not only disgrace but incredible mischief in burning several of our best Men O War lying at anchor and moored there . . . this alarm was so great, as put both country and City into a panic: fear and consternation such as I hope I shall never see more: for everybody was fleeing, none knew why or whither.

June 13:

Every able-bodied man in the City ordered to enlist: Charles II hurriedly reviews City Militia on Tower Hill.[9]

July 31:

Treaty of Breda ends Second Dutch War.

Dec 19:

Pepys: I to the Guildhall . . . and did look up and down this place where I have not been since the Fire, and see that the City are got a pace on in the rebuilding of Guildhall.

By the end of 1667, some 150 new houses had been built.

*51. London's new
brick buildings were
built to standard
designs. This elegant
house in Botolph Lane
(now demolished) was
of the fourth sort, 'of
the greatest bigness'*

52. Stationers' Hall. The City Companies had to rebuild their halls with whatever funds they could muster. Stationers' Hall was finished c1670

1668:

Samuel Rolle: Is London a village that I see, the houses in it stand so scatteringly? The major part of houses built upon the ruins let out to alehouse keepers and victuallers to entertain the workmen employed about the City . . . A goodly uniformity there is in so much of it as is built together, but ruins and confusion round about it . . . Few expect to trade within the walls (so far as the ruins do extend) till the City be built again . . . and therefore though they have built houses for themselves . . . yet do they refrain to go to them till their neighbourhood be increased.[10]

A further 1450 new houses built; Halls for the Butchers, Cutlers and Innholders.

1669:

Another 2,350 houses built; halls for the Plaisterers, Pewterers, Goldsmiths and Painter-stainers; riverstairs at Billingsgate and Puddle Dock repaired.

Evelyn: To London, spending almost the entire day in surveying what progress was made in rebuilding the ruinous City which now began a little to revive after its sad calamity.

1670:

Another 2,050 houses built; halls for the Curriers, Stationers, Fishmongers, Watermen, Saddlers; work begins on thirteen new churches. New market sites prepared at the Stocks, Honey Lane and Newgate[11]

53. The second Royal Exchange. *The new building was open for business in September 1669. It was destroyed by fire again in 1838*

Opposite:
54. The rebuilt Custom House. *The new Custom House was completed in 1671, but was badly damaged by fire in January 1715 when a neighbouring building in which gunpowder was sold, was accidentally blown up*

55. West View of Blackwell Hall, King Street, Cheapside. *(Publ. 1820). This market for woollen cloths was rebuilt by 1672.*

1671:
Another 1,100 houses built.

Evelyn: Returning home, I went on shore to see Custom House, now newly built since the dreadful conflagration.

Rebuilt Guildhall used for Lord Mayor's Feast in November. The Royal Exchange and Blackwell Hall completed; halls for the Vintners, Drapers, Coopers, Parish Clerks and Skinners; repairs to the river stairs at Queenhithe, Trig Lane and the Old Swan. Work begins on four new churches, on the Fleet Canal, and, in Fish Street Hill, on the Monument to the late dreadful Fire. Second Rebuilding Act passed by Parliament.

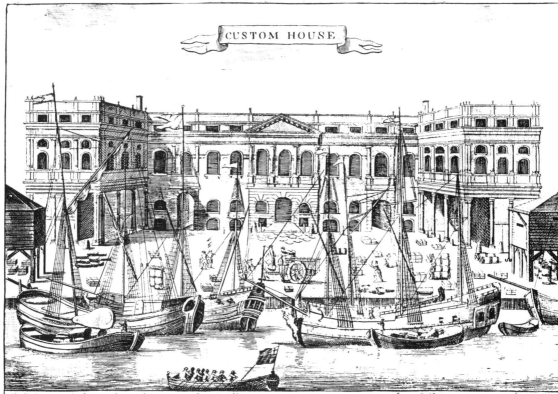

CUSTOM HOUSE

The Custom House for the Port of London, or Grand Office for the Management not only of the Affairs relating to ij Exports and Imports of this Opulent City; but of the Customs throughout England, according to the Regulation of Parliament. It was built by K. Charles the 2.d Anno 1668, at the Expence of above 10,000 Pounds, the former House being consumed by the Fire of London. It is a large and gracefull Building, fronting the Water side, very Comodious as well for the Commissioners and the several Officers and Clerks above Stairs, as the Ware houses underneath, and the Cranes for Landing and Lading the Merch.ts Goods. &c.

1672–1711: RESTORED TO GREATER BEAUTY
1672:

Another 600 houses built; Doctors' Commons, gaols at Wood Street, Poultry, Ludgate and Newgate completed; halls for the Apothecaries, Mercers, Founders and Tallow Chandlers. Reclamation on the waterfront at Blackfriars and Whitefriars; repairs to the river stairs at Blackfriars and Three Cranes; work begins on one new church.

Equestrian statute of Polish King John Sobieski overcoming a Turk converted into a likeness of Charles II overcoming Oliver Cromwell in a turban: it was erected in the Stocks Market (present day Mansion House).[12]

1673:

Another 200 houses built; work on one church completed – St Vedast, Foster Lane. Hall for the Merchant Taylors.

Census reveals that 1,000 plots still unbuilt, and 3,500 houses unoccupied.

1674:

Another 100 houses built; Fleet Canal completed; work begins on three new churches and on clearing the site of St Paul's.

1675:

Foundation stone for St Paul's Cathedral laid on June 21. One church completed – St Christopher-le-Stocks.

1676:

Two churches completed – St Mary-at-Hill and St Dionis Backchurch; work begins on three new churches.

May 26:

A great fire destroys a substantial part of Southwark, the City's southern suburb.

1677:

The publication of the Ogilby and Morgan survey of London, the *London Directory* (a list of London's merchants and bankers), and William Leybourn's *Survey of the Public Markets of the City*.[13]

The Monument and one church completed – St Michael Cornhill. One church repaired, St Mary Woolnoth; work begins on eight new churches.

1678:

Work on one new church begins.

Scandal of Titus Oates and the alleged Popish Plot to assassinate the King.

1679:

As a result of this anti-Catholic mood, the Lord Mayor of London arranged for an additional inscription on the Monument, which read 'The burning of this protestant City was begun and carried on by the treachery and malice of the Popish faction, in order to the effecting their horrid plot for the extirpating the protestant religion and to introduce Popery and heresey'. Edward Coleman, a court Catholic, and several Jesuits were executed. Samuel Pepys temporarily imprisoned in the Tower, suspected of selling naval secrets to the French.

Four churches completed – St Olave Jewry, St Mildred Poultry, St Edmund King and Martyr, and St George's Botolph Lane.

Jan 26:

Fire destroys many buildings near Middle Temple Lane, off Fleet Street.

56. *In 1689, following the accession of the Protestant King William and Mary to the English throne, an inscription was added to the base of the Monument stating that the 'most dreadful burning of this Protestant City was begun and carried on by the treachery and malice of the Popish faction . . .' Such was the continuing distrust of Catholics that these inflammatory words were not erased until 1831, by which time Catholics had finally won the right to sit in Parliament.*

57. The Old and the New: a typical example of a pre-Fire timber building, with projecting upper storeys, standing next to a smart brick building made to the regulations of the post-Fire legislation, with the characteristic brick bands at each floor level.

Opposite:
58. The College of Arms. The College was automatically rebuilt by 1680 and parts of it survive today, although the southern range was destroyed when Queen Victoria Street was laid out

59. The Execution of Monmouth, July 15, 1685. (From a contemporary Dutch print). The emnity between Protestants and Papists burned unabated in the late 17th century. In 1685, the Monmouth Rebellion was ended with his execution on Tower Hill. In spite of such political upheavals, the rebuilding of London continued

1680–4:
College of Arms and five churches completed – St Bride's, St Nicholas Cole Abbey, St Stephen Cleman, St Michael Bassishaw, St Benet Fink; repairs to St Mary Aldermary and St Augustine & St Faiths.
Work began on eleven new churches.

1682:
Nov 19:
Fire in Wapping destroys 1,000 houses and boats in Wapping Dock. 40–50 people killed.
1683:
Evelyn: June 23: After the Popish Plot etc there was now a new . . . Protestant Plot, that certain lords and others should design the assassination of his Majesty and the Duke of York (who had admitted being a Catholic) as they were come from Newmarket with a general rising of several of the nation, especially the City of London.
However, the Rye House Plot was discovered and the ringleaders were sent to Tower.

Prospect des Thur-hils zu Londen worauff der Hertzog von Monmuth den 5t July 1685 enthaubt worden.

1685:

Death of Charles II: accession of his brother the catholic Duke of York, James II.

Evelyn: June 17 . . . The Duke of Monmouth invaded this nation . . . which wonderfully alarmed the whole kingdom, fearing the joining of disaffected people . . . He had at his landing charged His Majesty with usurpation and several horrid crimes . . . The Duke was proclaimed a traitor. Now were also those words in the inscription about the Monument (implicating the papists in the burning of the City) erased and cut out.

July 6:

Monmouth's army defeated at the Battle of Sedgemoor, and the rebellion forcibly put down.

1686:

A Catholic chapel was opened in Lime Street, causing a riot in the City.[14]

1687:

Catholic chapels were opened in Bucklersbury, Savoy, St John's Clerkenwell and Lincoln's Inn Fields. Jesuit School opened at the Savoy.

1688:

A Jesuit school opened in Lime Street was scene of riots in October and November.

Nov 5:

The Revolution: the protestant William of Orange and his army landed in

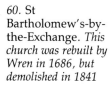

60. St Bartholomew's-by-the-Exchange. *This church was rebuilt by Wren in 1686, but demolished in 1841*

Devon, and began the long march to London.

Dec 11:

On Tuesday night there was an alarm occasioned by the burning of the Papist's chapels in London . . . having levelled them, the Londoners visited Henry Hill's printing house which they served in like manner.

On this night, James II fled from London, having burnt the writs for Parliament, disbanded the army and pitched the great seal in the river.

1689:

William and Mary proclaimed King and Queen.

The inscription on the Monument implicating the catholics in the Great Fire of London re-inscribed.

1685–9:

Twenty-four churches completed – St Lawrence Jewry, St Magnus Martyr, St Stephen Walbrook, St Bartholomew Exchange, St James Garlickhithe, St Michael Queenhithe, St Anne & St Agnes, St Swithins, St Peters Cornhill, All Hallows the More, All Hallows Bread Street, St Benets Paul's Wharf, St Martin Ludgate, St Mary Abchurch, St Mildred Bread Street, St Benet Gracechurch Street, St Mathew Friday Street, St Alban Wood Street, St Mary Magdelen Old Fish Street, St Clement Eastcheap, St Margaret Pattens, St Michael Crooked Lane, St Michael Wood Street, St Mary Aldermanbury.

Work on five new churches begins.

1690–5:

Seven churches completed – Christchurch Newgate Street, St Antholins Watling Street, St Andrew-by-the-Wardrobe, St Michael Pasternoster, Allhallows Lombard Street, St Mary Somerset, St Margaret Lothbury.

The Bank of England was established.

1698:

Jan 4:

Fire destroys many buildings in Whitehall.

1702:

William III dies; accession of Queen Anne.

Work begins on the dome of St Paul's Cathedral.

1706–8:

The western towers of St Paul's built.

1711:

St Paul's Cathedral completed.

The main sources for this chapter are T. F. Reddaway, *The Rebuilding of London after the Great Fire* (1940) and P. E. Jones & T. F. Reddaway (eds), *The Survey of building sites in the City of London after the Great Fire of 1666, by Peter Mills & John Oliver,* London Topographcial Society No 103 (1967).

For a detailed rebuttal of the claim that Wren's plan for rebuilding the City drawn up in 1666 was unfairly rejected 'by the narrow selfishness of its citizens', see Reddaway (1940) Appendix A, pp 311-2.

The **Diary of Redevelopment** also draws on the Diaries of Evelyn and Pepys and the *Calendar of State Papers Domestic* (see Notes in Part Two), while more detailed information on 17th-century buildings in London came from N. Pevsner, *The Buildings of England: London, Vol 1* (1973) and the Royal Commission for Historical Monuments, *An Inventory of the Historical Monuments in London: Vol IV, the City* (1929).

[1] *Calendar State Papers Domestic 1666–7*, p. 175.

[2] P. E. Jones & T. F. Reddaway (1967): see introductory note.

[3] Anon, *The London Directory of 1667: the Oldest printed List of Bakers and Merchants in London* (reprinted 1878).

[4] N. Pevsner, *The Buildings of England: London Vol 1* (1973), p 63.

[5] T. Reddaway, *The Rebuilding of London* (1940), p 286; 300.

[6] A. Beier & R. Finlay, *The Making of the Metropolis: London 1500–1700* (1986), p. 3.

[7] *Journal Court Common Council*, 46, Fo 121, 123.

[8] *Calendar State Papers Domestic, 1666–7*, p 76.

[9] R. Weinstein, *A London Tankard and the Dutch Wars*, LAMAS, 34 (1981), pp 151–2.

[10] S. Rolle, *London's Resurrection, or the Rebuilding of London* (1668), pp 91–5.

[11] B. Masters, *The Public Markets of the City of London surveyed by Wm Leybourn in 1677*, London Topographical Society No 117 (1974).

[12] T. Murdoch, *The Lord Mayor's Procession of 1686*, LAMAS, 34 (1983), pp 207–12.

[13] A splendid facsimile edition of the Ogilby & Morgan Survey of London was published in 1976 by Harry Margary in association with the Guildhall Library, London. For the Leybourn survey of the markets, see Note 11.

[14] T. G. Holt, *A Jesuit School in the City in 1688*, LAMAS, 32 (1981), pp 153–8.

PART FOUR:

Archaeology and the Great Fire of London

The story presented so far has been based on the documented history of the Fire compiled from written sources. This picture has now been augmented by archaeological research, which is concerned with the study of the actual physical remains of the past. For example a number of excavations have recently been conducted by archaeologists from the Museum of London on sites of this period in advance of their imminent redevelopment.[1] As a result, buildings and material lost in the Fire were recorded. Obviously such discoveries provide a physical reality that even Thomas Vincent's eloquence cannot match. Archaeologists working in the 20th century are able to photograph buildings which were destroyed over 300 years ago. Some of the illustrations in this book are of structures which were last seen in September 1666, after which they were burnt, covered and forgotten. Such photographs provide a dramatic dimension to our understanding of that catastrophe.

Studying London's Buildings
Of equal importance is the detailed study of those buildings and the associated finds, from which much can be learned of the layout and life of London at that time, and in the preceding period. Although major fires in towns were disastrous for the contemporary inhabitants, they are often, perversely, a considerable benefit to latter-day archaeologists. This is because after such a fire destroys the superstructure of a building, the outline of the foundations (ie the plan of the structure) is frequently left well-preserved under a thick debris layer laid over the site before rebuilding began. In this way a clear idea is obtained of the form of the destroyed building, albeit scorched, charred or blackened, but nevertheless frozen at a moment in time. The layers which filled the cellars of buildings burnt in the Great Fire were often very thick, and, as a result, archaeologists have been able to examine structures and finds thought lost in the Fire. In addition, substantial fragments of medieval churches, such as St Peter's in Upper Thames Street and St Botolph, Billingsgate have also been discovered, together with the cobbled lanes and remains of neighbouring buildings.[2] The structure sealed by Great Fire debris on a site excavated by Tim Williams in Lime Street in 1984 was of especial interest, for

61. Archaeological excavations at Pudding Lane in the shadow of the Monument revealed part of a building burnt down on 2nd September, 1666

the cellar incorporated a substantial proportion of a Roman masonry building, which therefore may have been in use for over 1,500 years.[3]

Not all the Museum's work has been underground, for Richard Lea has spent much time examining standing buildings in the City. In 1984 he was monitoring the repairs to the roof of St Mary-at-Hill, a church thought to have been destroyed in the Fire and rebuilt to Wren's design from 1670–76, with a new tower added in 1730. However, when the plaster rendering on the north wall was stripped off, the original pre-Fire masonry was revealed, standing to its full height. Wren's circular brick window had simply been inserted into a

62. Restoration work at St Mary-at-Hill in Lovat Lane. *When the rendering was stripped from this building, it was found that Wren's design incorporated much of the older stonework from the medieval church. Wren's circular brick window – just above the danger sign – was inserted into a larger infilled medieval window set in the original stone wall*

larger blocked-up stone window. The 'new' church was therefore a careful adaptation of whatever fragments of serviceable masonry walling had survived the Fire: clearly it had been designed in the field. Such activity is mirrored on several other sites. The west wall of St Martin's Ludgate incorporated a 17m-high section of the Roman city wall for example, while the foundations of the late 17th century Christchurch in Newgate Street were deliberately built directly over the stable footings of the medieval church of Greyfriars.[4] Wren's churches, like so much of the post-Fire City, had all the

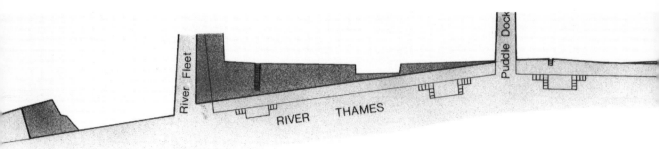

63. In 1671, a design was drawn up to extend and straighten the indented late-medieval Thames waterfront to form the New Quay. But was the plan actually carried out? This drawing of the west end of the City quay shows the indented pre-Fire waterfront line to the north, in front of which the darker shaded areas mark land reclaimed from the river after 1666; its southern edge is the waterfront planned on Ogilby and Morgan's Survey of 1677. The other line marks the alignment of the proposed New Quay, complete with elaborate river stairs. Clearly the plan for the New Quay was subjected to considerable modification between the drawing board and the riverside

outward appearances of late 17th century design, but retained the medieval plan.

More prosaic evidence for the rebuilding of London comes from the frequent discovery of 17th century quarries which had been dug outside the suburbs of the City to make the bricks for the new town. A cargo of these locally-made bricks was actually found on the remains of a boat which had sunk in the Thames near Blackfriars.[5] Water transport would also have been required in quantity for the shipment of the 50,322 tons of stone from Portland for St Paul's Cathedral. That island was transformed by new quarries, roads and jetties, evidence of which is still visible today, as the rebuilding of London made its mark over a wide area of England. Indeed even Scandinavia was visibly affected by the unprecedented demand for building materials, since the native British woodlands were unable to provide all the timber urgently needed for London's floors and roofs. It was suggested that 'The Norwegians warmed themselves comfortably by the Fire of London'.[6]

On the Waterfront

Part of a recent study of the London waterfront affords an interesting example of the profitable integration of documentary, cartographic and archaeological research. The Ogilby and Morgan survey shows the line of the newly-completed Fleet Canal and the broad, open New Quay along the Thames. The first of these two projects is known to have been undertaken from 1671–4, and proved a more difficult task than Christopher Wren had anticipated. Fortunately, Thomas Fitch was able to improve the design for the brick retaining walls and completed the project.[7] Part of the works associated with that scheme were uncovered during an excavation in 1984 supervised by Prince Chitwood in New Bridge Street. Several metres to the east, on the landward side of the Fleet, he also found a spectacular length of the medieval wall marking the line of the earlier river bank. The area between the old and new banks had been reclaimed in the late 17th century by infilling it with building debris derived from the clearance of fire-damaged structures.[8]

A similar situation was encountered just 100m to the south, when Ken Steedman examined part of the New Quay in 1985, during the redevelopment of Blackfriars Underground station.[9] Once again, a massive medieval river-wall survived in fine condition and, extending over the sandy foreshore into what had been the open river, was a mass of burnt debris from the Great Fire.

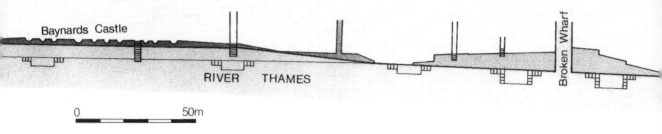

Although the late 17th century river wall was not located in this archaeological excavation, its line can be seen on the Ogilby and Morgan survey. Once again, the area between the two frontages had been reclaimed by utilising some of the vast amount of debris that Londoners had cleared from their building plots and streets and dumped on the waterfront.

As a result of such waterfront extensions, London was not only able to rid itself of much of its destruction debris, but was also actually larger after the Great Fire than it was before. It is now possible to measure the extent of this substantial encroachment on part of London's waterfront by plotting the line of the pre-Fire waterfront onto the Ogilby and Morgan survey. A detailed plan of line of the waterfront dated to 1671, ie before the late 17th century encroachments took place, was examined in the Corporation of London Records Office (Charter 98).[10] It shows that the pre-Fire river front took an irregular course and was much indented. In this respect it mirrored the older medieval pattern revealed in the excavations at Billingsgate and Trig Lane for example.[11] In addition, the plan is marked with another line representing proposed improvements, incorporating considerable encroachments to provide a more uniform, straighter waterfront. Since the actual orientation and alignment of the plan was uncertain, it was not known exactly where the pre-Fire waterfront line was in relation to the present-day river bank, or how much of the proposed scheme was actually carried out. However, as a result of the recent archaeological excavations, the line of the pre-Fire waterfront has now been exposed and accurately plotted on several occasions, and the extent of the post-Fire reclamation established for at least part of the London waterfront.

Finds from the Fire

Apart from coins, few ancient artefacts are discovered with a date neatly marked upon them. From the Museum of London collections, a short catalogue of some post-medieval pottery has been published and a recent discovery of a pewter pot which could be connected with the Second Dutch War[12] are some of the more interesting exceptions that prove the rule. However, much of the material recovered from the Museum's Great Fire excavations can be associated with events in the 1660s to 1670s. These closely-dated deposits clearly have significant implications for the study of 17th-century sites elsewhere in this country and also in former British colonies, such as those in

64. This 5 × 100mm
scale sits on the
foreshore at the foot of
the medieval river wall
on the west bank of the
Fleet River. After the
Fire the land to the
west was reclaimed
when the Fleet was
canalised, and the face
of this 3m high wall
was sealed beneath a
vast dump of debris
cleared from the burnt
City. In 1984,
archaeologists
working in New
Bridge Street recorded
it before it was
destroyed by
redevelopment

America, where similar finds may have been discovered from an otherwise undatable context. For this reason material from the City associated with the Great Fire of London is being brought together for publication by Dr Alan Vince and his colleagues in the Museum of London. The range of material involved is considerable and includes many types of pottery, glass, tiles, and tobacco pipes.

An Excavation in Pudding Lane

This short survey of archaeological research related to the Great Fire will conclude with a brief report on a recent excavation, to show how the results of such investigations can enhance the historical record. The property in question was on a site very close to the infamous bakehouse in which the Fire actually started.[13] The excavations in the winter of 1979/80 exposed a cellar fronting onto Pudding Lane, in which barrels of pitch were being stored at the time of the Fire.

The brick-lined cellar had been resurfaced in the early 17th-century. The bricks had to be cut to butt flush against the south wall of the cellar, demonstrating that the floor was laid from north to south, and that the cellar did not form a perfect rectangle in plan. The level of the surface undulated with the major depressions overlying areas of early medieval pitting showing that the floor must have been operative long enough for such subsidence to take place. The bricks did not appear to be reused, but some ten per cent showed signs of wear consistent with the installation and use of tables or racks rather than the passage of feet. Although this cellar was floored and faced with brick, the building it served was almost certainly timber-framed. Such a combination of brick or stone cellar beneath a timber superstructure is known elsewhere in London[14] and in other towns, such as Norwich, Southampton and Chester.

Directly overlying the floor was a mass of moderately compacted carbonised material representing features burnt *in-situ*. After careful dissection of the deposit, it was possible to identify the remains of some twenty barrels closely-bound with wooden hoops, which had been stored on five racks. The best preserved elements of these structures were in the south-west corner of the area and these justify detailed description.

At least three undressed parallel carbonised timber poles lay horizontally east-west: the longest fragment was 2.1m long and all were 50mm in diameter, and were cut from trees at least ten years old. The largest member was overlain by four groups of up to sixteen carbonised hoop fragments. Each fragment was up to 30mm wide and 500mm long, was D-shaped in cross-section, and had been cut from coppiced sweet chestnut. They lay curved face downwards, aligned east-west but with their east and west ends raised, forming a slight concave profile.

Each group was directly overlain by more substantial timbers representing the barrel staves themselves, which were also carbonised. The most westerly assemblage comprised two sets of oak stave fragments all aligned north-south, conforming to the east-west concave profile of the underlying hoops. Three of the more northerly group of four fragments seemed to be part of the

*Opposite:
65. This cellar in Pudding Lane was filled with debris from fire-damaged buildings. Since this event is known to have taken place in September 1666, archaeologists excavating such deposits are able to date associated artefacts like these glazed tiles very closely*

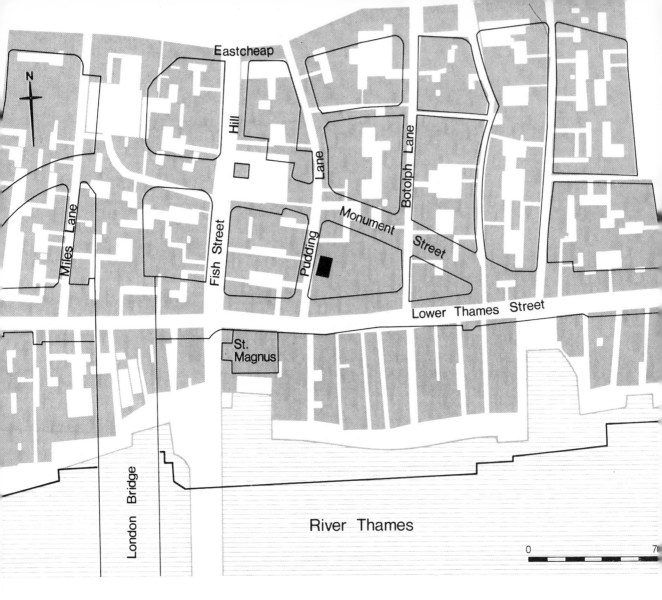

Eastcheap

Hill Lane

Botolph Lane

Miles Lane

Fish Street

Pudding

Monument

Street

Lower Thames Street

St. Magnus

London Bridge

River Thames

0   70

66. Location of the
1979–80 excavations
in Pudding Lane in
relation to the
modern street plan.
*The toned area
represents the street
pattern shown on
Ogilby and Morgan's
Survey of 1677.
Although approach
roads to London
Bridge are much
altered, some of the
other lanes still follow
their 17th-century
alignments. (C.
Milne)*

same staves as the southern fragments, from which it was deduced that they would have originally been some 0.92m long. The staves were 110mm wide, tapering to 90mm at both ends, which were chamfered and cut by the V-shaped groove characteristic of barrel staves.

Several similar groups of barrel fragments were recorded, usually aligned north-south on racks aligned east-west. All the barrels seemed to be of the same size and type, each 0.9m long, comprising up to fourteen staves closely-bound with wooden hoops around a cask with a diameter of 1.5m in the middle, tapering to 1.25m at the ends.

All these features were covered by the tar-like substance once contained in the barrels. It had formed a hard crust on the upper surface of the blackened brickwork and had percolated between the bricks, staining their sides and discolouring the earlier surfaces beneath. Miscroscopic analysis of samples taken from this deposit was conducted by the British Carbonisation Research Association. It concluded that the carbonaceous material had the open spherical structure associated with the later stages of carbonisation of pitch.[15] In Northern Europe, resinous woods such as pine, larch or fir were burnt in a controlled supply of air inadequate to allow complete combustion so that the tar which then oozed from the wood could be collected. This impure form of resin, known as 'Stockholm Tar' could be used for waterproofing, although further distillation would produce 'wood pitch', a substance which was more viscous than tar and was often of more value for waterproofing (Hodges 1964). It is suggested that it was this commodity, wood pitch, which was stored in the Pudding Lane cellar at the time of the fire. This compound cannot have been derived directly from the burning of the barrel staves themselves, since they were cut from non-resinous oak.

Over this layer had been dumped mixed deposits of bricks, tiles, mortar and other material, some of which showed signs of burning and vitrification. They represent the debris from the clearance or collapse of fire-damaged structures. The presence of over 100 whole stock-moulded bricks in these dumps suggests that the debris had not been sorted. Analysis has shown that there were also fragments of roof tile of the standard peg tile form characteristic of local manufacture from the late fifteenth century. Many had been badly burnt, contorted and warped by the fire, and some fragments had exploded with the intensity of the heat. Molten and twisted nails were mixed in with the building debris, as were fragments of window glass, metal objects possibly representing iron brackets of varying sizes, part of a pivot, a hinge and a lock. Four fragments of badly burned and partially vitrified stove tiles were also recovered, on which a moulded figure of a Triton (merman) was identified.

Many broken earthenware storage jars of a hitherto unknown type were also found in these deposits, as were two unused tin-glazed polychrome tiles which had fallen so that their lower edges were just over the scorched cellar floor. Only this edge of the tiles were burnt, which suggests that at least some of the debris was introduced into the cellar while the fire was still smouldering, and cannot therefore have been brought from a great distance.

That the function of the building could be deduced from examination of the contents of the cellar and of its infill material is also of interest. Clearly the presence of so many barrels on racks shows that the cellar was used as a store, and the analysis of the contents shows that it was probably 'pitch in the later stages of carbonisation'.[15] The pitch would have been a by-product of wood-tar, produced when making charcoal, and was extensively used for such projects as the waterproofing of ship's hulls (the cellar was only 100m from Billingsgate, a major harbour in the seventeenth century). The material in the dumped deposits overlying the barrel fragments not only contained the remains of many identical earthenware storage jars, but also large quantities of metal hooks and eyes contorted by the heat. This implies that the premises above the cellar may have been used as a shop.

The dating evidence may be summarised thus: pottery found in the levels beneath the cellar floor can be dated no earlier than the 15th century. The brick floor itself had clearly been in use for some time before the Fire, as its worn appearance and the considerable subsidence demonstrates. The large

assemblage from the deposits which sealed it have been argued to represent material burnt *in-situ* or dumped very shortly after a conflagration and therefore can be assumed to be broadly contemporary. As a result, it is possible to propose a much closer date for this phase.

The associated finds included a very worn sixpence of Elizabeth I (1558-1603); clay tobacco pipes of the types usually dated 1660-80; local lead glazed monochrome floor tiles and (?Dutch) tin glazed polychrome tiles of types usually dated to the late sixteenth-early seventeenth century and the neck and shoulder of a glass 'wine' bottle of a type introduced in *c* 1650. In addition, radio-carbon determinations of 1685 ± 70 and 1640 ± 70 were obtained from the carbonised fragments of barrel staves and hoops. Taken together, it seems reasonable to assume that that the cellar was resurfaced with bricks in the early seventeenth century, and that the conflagration which destroyed it was that of September 1666.

Fires were very common in medieval London, but they were usually small or localised. What made the the Great Fire of 1666 so devastating was that it started in the waterfront area where large quantities of combustible material were stored. It was the proximity of such fire hazards as timber-framed warehouses with cellars full of pitch barrels to the infamous bakehouse that turned what could have been just another minor fire into a major catastrophe. Although the pitch barrels recorded in the excavation did not start the blaze, they did provide fuel for it. Without that, the fire in Pudding Lane might have burnt itself out unremarked on Sunday 2nd September, 1666.

Opposite:
67. Charred remains of pitch barrels lying on the scorched brick floor of a cellar destroyed on Sunday, 2nd September, 1666. Scale 2 × 100mm

68. The staves of these burnt barrels were held in place with closely-bound wooden hoops: scale 2 × 100mm

[1] Summaries of the Museum of London's excavations are published in the spring issues of *The London Archaeologist* (LA) and in *Popular Archaeology* (Pop Arch); more detailed reports in the *Transactions of the London and Middlesex Archaeological Society* (LAMAS), while the complete archive reports are housed in the Museum of London library, where they may be consulted by request.
[2] T. Williams, *St Peter's Hill*, Pop Arch (July 1982), pp 24–30; *Billingsgate Lorry park, Lower Thames Street*, LA 4 No 10 (1983), p 274.
[3] T. Williams, *Excavations at 25–6 Lime Street*, LA 4 No 16 (1984), pp 426–30.
[4] R. Lea, *The Archaeology of standing structures in the City of London*, Pop Arch (Jan 1986), pp 22–30; for St Martin's Church see LA 4 No 10 (1983), p 275; P. Herbert, *Excavations at Christchurch Greyfriars, 1976*, LA 3 No 12 (1979), pp 327–32.
[5] P. Marsden, *A 17th-century boat found in London*, Post-Medieval Archaeology 5 (1971), pp 88–98.
[6] T. Reddaway, *The Rebuilding of London*, (1940), p 121.
[7] *Ibid*, chapter viii.
[8] *New Bridge Street*, LA 5, No 2 (1985), p 49.
[9] *167–77 Queen Victoria Street*, LA 5, No 6 (1986), p 161.
[10] S. Perks, *The Waterline of the City of London after the Great Fire* (1935); T. Reddaway (see Note 6), pp 231–5.
[11] G. Milne & C. Milne, *Medieval Waterfront Development at Trig Lane, London* LAMAS Special Paper No 5 (1982).
[12] F. Celoria, *Dated Post-medieval Pottery* HMSO (1966); R. Weinstein *A London tankard and the Dutch Wars* LAMAS 32 (1982), pp 151–2.
[13] G. Milne, *Archaeology and the Great Fire of London* Pop Arch (December 1983), pp 32–6; G. Milne & C. Milne, *A Building in Pudding Lane burnt in the Great Fire of London* LAMAS (forthcoming).
[14] L. F. Salzman, *Building in England down to 1540* (1952) Appendix B, Nos 15, 49, 51.
[15] Copy of report by D. Briggs of the British Carbonization Research Association in Museum of London library (PEN 79).
[16] H. Hodges, *Artefacts* (1964), 423–30.

APPENDIX 1:

Legislation for the new London

Two important acts were brought before Parliament in February 1667. Without them the complex rebuilding programme could not have begun, and these acts are summarised below. The first one (18–19 Chas 11, 7), established the Fire Court, the body which was concerned with the many and various property disputes arising out of the proposed redevelopment. It was initially estimated that it could complete its business by the end of the following year: in the event, such was the complexity of its task that the life of the Fire Court was extended until 1676. The planners of the new London had to face up to very considerable legal problems, a fact which is not often appreciated today. A reading of the Fire Court Act outlines the extent of that problem and helps to explain why a more radical replanning of the City was just not possible in the late 1660s.

The second measure (18–19 Chas II, 8) is concerned with the specifics of the rebuilding programme, and deals in considerable detail with matters ranging from extensive road-widening schemes to the provision of drain pipes and gutters for buildings. This Act represents the most comprehensive development plan the City had ever seen. An examination of these two important documents therefore helps to explain why London developed the way it did after the Fire, and that it was most certainly and effectively planned down to the last brick. The new London did not represent 'a wasted opportunity'.

In 1671, an additional act for the rebuilding of the City 'uniting of Parishes, rebuilding of the Cathedral and Parish Churches of the said City' (22 Chas II, 11) was passed. This modified or extended various provisions in the first Rebuilding Act, and introduced the other matters stated in the title. It also included measures concerning the Thames and Fleet Quays (Sections XXXVIII-XLII), and notes that 51 parishes churches would be required in the new City, rather than the 39 suggested in the 1667 act, or the 109 that had graced the City on 3rd September 1666. (The Second Rebuilding Act of 1671 is not summarised in any further detail in this appendix).

An Act for erecting a Judicature for Determination of Differences touching Houses burned or demolished in the late Fire which happened in London (18–19 Chas II, 7).

I Whereas the greatest part of the houses in the City of London and some of the suburbs thereof have been burnt by the dreadful and dismal Fire, many of the tenants, undertenants or late occupiers whereof are liable unto suits and actions to compel them to repair and rebuild the same and to pay their rents as if the same had not been burned, and are not relievable therein in any course of law, and great differences are like to arise concerning the said repairs and new building and payment of rents, which, if they should not be determined with all speed and without charge, would much obstruct the rebuilding of the City. And for that it is just that everyone concerned should bear a proportionable share of the loss according to their several interests, since no general rule can be prescribed, be it therefore enacted that the Justice of the Courts of the Kings Bench and Common Pleas and the Barons of the Coife in the Exchequer or any three or more of them sitting at the same time and place are hereby authorised to hear and determine all differences and demands whatsoever which have arisen or may arise

1) between landlords, proprietors, tenants, lessees, undertenants or late occupiers of any of the said buildings with their appurtenances or

2) any person having or claiming any estate, right, title or interest in the same, or

3) any other persons concerning the repairing, building or rebuilding of the said houses or any other grounds lying within that part of the City lately ruined by reason of the said Fire, or

4) concerning the payment or abatement of any rent other than the arrears of rent due before the Fire (the Judges) shall and may upon the verdict of jurors, testimony of witnesses upon oath, examination of interested parties, according to their discretions proceed to the hearing and determining of the demands and differences between the said parties and there shall be no appeal or review for the removal or reversal of the same.

II (The judges) shall have had authority to order

1) the surrender, increase, abridging, ceasing, determining or changing of any estate;

2) new or longer leases not exceeding 40 years at such rents or fines as they shall think fit.

III And for the better enabling (the judges) shall issue notes and warrants warning the person or persons therein named and concerned in the said complaint to appear before them.

IV The judgements and determinations which shall be made betwixt party and party by authority of this Act shall be recorded in a book or books which shall be placed in the custody of the Lord Mayor and Aldermen of the City unto which all persons concerned shall or may view.

V (The judges) are hereby enabled to order a table of such reasonable fees to be made.

An Act for the Rebuilding of the City of London
(18–19 Chas II, 8)

I For as much as the City of London by reason of a most dreadful fire was for the most part thereof burnt down and now lies buried in its own ruins, for the speedy restoration whereof and for the better regulation, uniformity and gracefulness of such new buildings as shall be erected, and to the end that great and outrageous fires may be reasonably prevented and that all encouragement and expedition may be given and all impediments and obstructions removed, be it therefore enacted that the rules and directions hereafter in this Act prescribed be duly observed by all persons therein concerned.

First, that no building for habitation be hereafter erected within the City unless it conforms to the rules and orders of building prescribed in this present Act, (otherwise) the builder thereof shall be committed to the common gaol till he shall have abated or demolished the same.

II That irregular buildings may be better prevented, the City shall elect one or more discreet and intelligent person or persons knowledgeable in the art of building to see the said rules well and truly observed.

III There shall be only four sorts of building: first and least sort fronting by-lanes, second sort fronting streets and lanes of note, the third sort fronting high and principal streets. The roofs of each shall be uniform. The fourth and largest sort of mansion houses for citizens or other persons of extraordinary quality not fronting the three former ways.

IV The Lord Mayor shall on or before the 1st April 1667 declare which and how many streets shall hereafter be deemed by-lanes, streets or lanes of note, or high and principal streets. All the said streets intended to be rebuilt shall be marked and staked out (so that) the breadth, length and extent thereof shall be better known and observed. (The penalty for moving or removing these stakes was three months imprisonment or £10, or, if the offence was committed by a person of low and mean condition, that he shall be openly whipped till his body be bloody).

V That all the outsides of buildings be henceforth made of brick or stone.

VI Party walls to be set out equally on each builder's ground: to be built up by the first beginner of such building, and convenient toothing to be left in the front wall for the better joining of the next house.

VII–IX Proportions of first, second and third sort of houses specified.
(see Table below)

Table showing proportions of the new sorts of buildings

SORT OF BUILDING	STOREY	HEIGHT OF STOREY	THICKNESS OF FRONT & REAR WALLS	THICKNESS OF WALLS BETWEEN HOUSES
FIRST	Cellar	6ft 6ins	2 bricks	1½ bricks
	1st	9ft	1½ bricks	1½ bricks
	2nd	9ft	1½ bricks	1½ bricks
	Garret		1 brick	1 brick
SECOND	Cellar	6ft 6ins	2½ bricks	2 bricks
	1st	10ft	2 bricks	1½ bricks
	2nd	10ft	2 bricks	1½ bricks
	3rd	9ft	1½ bricks	1½ bricks
	Garret			
THIRD	1st	10ft	2½ bricks	2 bricks
	2nd	10ft 6ins	1½ bricks	1½ bricks
	3rd	9ft	1½ bricks	1½ bricks
	4th	8ft 6ins	1½ bricks	1½ bricks
	Garret		1 brick	1 brick

X The fourth sort of building being mansion houses of the greatest bigness shall bear the same scantlings as in the Table, the number of stories and height thereof left to the discretion of the builder, so long as he exceed not four stories.

XI–XII In front of all houses erected in high streets, balconies 4 foot broad with rails and bars of iron shall be placed and water falling from the top of the said houses be conveyed into channels by pipes on the sides and fronts of houses. No jetties, windows or anything of the like sort shall be made to extend beyond the ancient foundation line of any house, save for the stall boards when their shop windows are set open.

XIII If any person with any ground which was formerly builded upon, the houses thereupon being burned or pulled down, shall not within three years build up the same, then the Mayor shall give notice to cause the same to be rebuilt within the nine months next following. And if the owners shall refuse or neglect to rebuild after inquiry and valuation thereof, it shall be lawful for the Mayor to make sale of the property.

XIV–XV And to the end that the said builders may receive due encouragement by having the materials for building at reasonable prices and getting of workmen for moderate wages, two judges of the Kings Bench may set the prices of bricks, tiles and mortar etc.

XVI That all carpenters, bricklayers, masons, plasterers, joiners and other artificers, workmen and labourers employed in the buildings who are not freemen of the City shall for the space of seven years [ie until 1674] or until all the said buildings shall be fully finished, have the same liberty as Freemen of the City.

XVII Differences arising between builders or any others concerning the stopping up of lights, windows, watercourses, gutters etc may be heard by the Alderman of the ward.

XVIII The number and places for all common sewers, drains and vaults and the manner of paving and pitching the streets and lanes shall be designed and set out by persons appointed by the Mayor.

XIX Trades and occupations judged noisome or perilous in respect of fire may be prohibited in the high and principal streets.

XX Conduits now standing in the high streets may be removed and erected in other public places.

XXI The Mayor empowered and required to enlarge Fleet Street, the street from east end of St Paul's into Cheapside, that from Cheapside into Poultry, that from Poultry to the west end of

Cornhill, Blowbladder Street, Newgate Street where the shambles lately stood, Ave Marie Lane, that from St Martin's Le Grande to Blowbladder Street, from St Magnus Church to Gracechurch Street, the north end of Gracechurch Street, Thames Street, Old Fish Street.

XXII   Mayor shall enlarge any other street or narrow passage less than 14 feet in breadth.

XXIII–XXV   Compensation payable to those who lost ground through such street widening schemes.

XXVI   The 2nd September be yearly for ever after observed as a day of public fasting and humiliation within the City and Liberties thereof to implore the mercies of Almighty God upon the said City to divert the like calamity for the time to come.

XXVII   The better to preserve the memory of this dreadful visitation, a column or pillar be erected on or as near unto the place where the said Fire so unhappily began, as conveniently be made in perpetual rememberance thereof.

XXVIII   That all traders of money formerly made at the late Royal Exchange now be made at Gresham House.

XXVIX–XXXI   That the parish churches to be rebuilt within the said City of London in lieu of those which were demolished by the late Fire shall not exceed the number of 39. [By 1671, it was decided that the number of churches rebuilt should be increased to 51].

XXXII–XXXIII   That for the prevention of innundations and for the easiness of ascent, Thames Street and all the ground between it and the River Thames shall be raised at the least by 3 foot above the surface of the ground as now it lieth, and no buildings shall be built within a distance of 40 feet from the Thames from the Tower to Temple Stairs, nor any house to be built within 40 foot of the middle of the River Fleet from the Thames to Clerkenwell on either side before the 24th March 1668.

XXXIV–XXXVIII   To enable the Mayor to perform and accomplish the work in this Act mentioned, that for all coals brought into London to be sold by the chaldron or tun, there shall be paid by way of imposition thereupon 12 pence for every tun paid unto the Mayor. Every such sum which shall be raised thus shall in the first place be applied for the satisfaction of such persons whose grounds be taken for the enlarging of the streets and for the making of wharves and quays on the North side of the Thames, on each side of the sewer called Fleet ditch and also for the building of prisons in the City.

There shall be kept in the Chamber of London books in which all monies thereupon received shall be set down.

XXXIX   Provisions for rebuilding in timber the waterhouse at London Bridge.

XL   The Mayor to open and enlarge several streets leading down to the Thames for the conveniencing of trade and better passage of carts.

APPENDIX 2:

Churches and the Great Fire of London

The Great Fire burnt 87 of London's 109 churches. These ancient buildings, representing the subdivision of the teeming capital into smaller parish communites, contributed much to the life of the City and its citizens. The remarkable density of churches in the medieval town is captured on 16th and early 17th-century views of the City, the skyline of which is dominated by the cluster of spires and towers. Of the 22 churches unharmed by the Fire, 13 survive to this day with at least some of their pre-Fire features intact, 5 have been rebuilt in the 18th or 19th centuries, and 4 have been demolished.

The Rebuilding Act of 1667 suggested that only 39 churches should be rebuilt, but the Second Rebuilding Act (1671) increased that number to 51. All the new churches were designed by Christopher Wren, and were built between 1670 and 1695, with the exception of St Paul's, upon which work continued until 1711. By that date London had 74 churches: today it has 42.

CHURCHES WHICH SURVIVED THE GREAT FIRE

Allhallows, Barking	Allhallows, London Wall
Allhallows, Staining	Tower of St Alphage, London Wall
St Andrew, Holborn	St Andrew Undershaft
St Bartholomew the Great	St Bartholomew the Less
St Botolph, Aldersgate	St Botolph, Aldgate
St Botolph, Bishopsgate	St Dunstan in the West
St Ethelburga	St Giles, Cripplegate
St Helen, Bishopsgate	(Holy Trinity Minories)
(St James, Dukes Place)	(St Katherine Coleman)
St Katherine Cree	(St Martin Outwich)
St Olave, Hart Street	St Peter ad Vincula

(churches marked with brackets now demolished)

CHURCHES DESTROYED IN THE GREAT FIRE AND NOT REBUILT

Allhallows the Less	Allhallows, Honey Lane
St Andrew Hubbard	St Anne Blackfriars
St Benet Sherehog	St Botolph Billingsgate
St Faith	St Gabriel Fenchurch
St Gregory-by-St Paul	Holy Trinity the Less
St John the Baptist	St John the Evangelist
St John Zachary	St Lawrence Pountney
St Leonard Eastcheap	St Leonard Foster Lane
St Margaret Moses	St Margaret Fish Street Hill
St Martin Orgar	St Martin Pomeroy
St Martin Vintry	St Mary Bothaw
St Mary Colechurch	St Mary Magdalen, Milk Street
St Mary Mounthaw	St Mary Staining
St Mary Woolchurch	St Michael le Querne

St Nicholas Acon	St Nicholas Olave	
St Olave, Silver Street	St Pancras, Soper Lane	
St Peter Chepe	St Peter, Paul's Wharf	
St Thomas the Apostle		

CHURCHES REBUILT AFTER THE GREAT FIRE, BUT SUBSEQUENTLY DESTROYED

Allhallows, Bread Street

Allhallows, Lombard Street

St Bartholomew Exchange

St Benet, Gracechurch Street

St Dionis Backchurch

St Mary Aldermanbury: rebuilt in Fulton,
   Missouri in the USA

St Mary Magdalen Old Fish Street

St Michael Bassishaw

St Michael, Queenhithe

St Mildred, Bread Street

St Peter-le-poore

St Swithin

Allhallows the More

St Antholin

St Benet Fink

St Christopher-le-Stocks

St George, Botolph Lane

St Mathew, Friday Street

St Michael, Crooked Lane

St Michael, Wood Street

St Mildred, Poultry

St Stephen, Coleman Street

CHURCHES REBUILT AFTER THE FIRE, SURVIVING TODAY

St Andrew-by-the-Wardrobe
St Benet Pauls Wharf
St Clement Eastcheap
St James Garlickhithe
St Magnus the Martyr
St Margaret Pattens
St Mary Abchurch
St Mary-le-bow
St Mary Woolnoth (rebuilt by Hawksmoor 1716–27)
St Michael Cornhill
St Nicholas Cole Abbey
St Peter, Cornhill
St Stephen Walbrook

St Anne & St Agnus
St Brides
St Edmund King & Martyr
St Lawrence Jewry
St Margaret Lothbury
St Martin Ludgate
St Mary Aldermary
St Mary-at-Hill

St Michael Paternoster Royal
St Pauls Cathedral
St Sepulchre
St Vedast, Foster Lane

TOWERS OR SHELL SURVIVING:

St Albans, Wood Street
Christchurch, Newgate Street
St Mary Somerset

St Augustine, Watling Street
St Dunstans-in-the-East
St Olave Jewry

70. London Rebuilt. By the early 18th century the wide City Streets were lined with elegant brick buildings and graceful churches, crowned by St Pauls. This view, showing St Bride's and Fleet Street, is by T. Bowles after J. Donowell.

2029.—A Parallel of some of the principal Towers and Steeples built by Sir Christopher Wren.

St. Dunstan in the East.   2, St. Magnus.   3, St. Benet, Gracechurch-street.   4, St. Edmund the King, Lombard Street.   5, St. Margaret Pattens.   6, Allhallows the Great.
7, St. Mary Abchurch.   8, St. Michael, Cornhill.   9, St. Lawrence, Jewry.   10, St. Benet Fink.   11, St. Bartholomew.   12, St. Michael, Queenhithe.   13. St. Michael Royal.
14, St. Antholin, Watling-street.   15, St. Stephen, Walbrook.   16, St. Swithin, Cannon-street.   17, St. Mary-le-bow.   18, Christ Church, Newgate-street.   19, St. Nicholas
Cole Abbey.   20, St. Mildred, Bread-street.   21, St. Augustin, Watling-street.   22, St. Mary Somerset.   23, St. Martin, Ludgate.   24, St. Andrew by the Wardrobe.
25, St. Bride, Fleet-street.

The Scale is expressed by St. Paul's in the background.

71. This plan,
published by Charles
Knight, shows the
towers of the churches
that Wren designed for
London.

123

INDEX